Waking Up
the Karma Fairy

Waking Up
the Karma Fairy

Life Lessons and Other Holy Adventures

Meg Barnhouse

Skinner House Books
Boston

Printed in Canada.

Cover design by Jill Feron.

Text design by WordCrafters.

Author photo by Susan M. Newton.

ISBN 1-55896-447-9

5   4   3   2   1

06   05   04   03

Library of Congress Cataloging-in-Publication Data

Barnhouse, Meg.
    Waking up the karma fairy : life lessons and other holy
  adventures / Meg Barnhouse.
      p. cm.
    ISBN 1-55896-447-9 (alk. paper)
      1. Spiritual life—Unitarian Universalist Association.   I. Title.

  BX9855.B37 2003
  248.4'891—dc21

                                                    2003041566

Contents

Prologue

༄

Sitting at the Center of the Universe, which is what we call the three pushed-together tables in the coffee shop where my friends and I meet in the morning, I asked, "Have you ever been bored with yourself?"

"What do you mean, bored with your job?" one friend asked.

"No. Not my job. Not my job or my love, or my family. Not with my friends. Those things are spicy, joyful, and bright. I've been bored with myself for the last four days. I'm tired of how I think, tired of everything I say, everything I wear, the way I see the world, tired of my approach to life."

"That's one step away from depression," another said. "You might need some Zoloft."

I don't feel depressed. In fact, I'm totally bored with the idea of being depressed. I'm bored with being mad, bored with being entertaining, bored with trying to figure things out. No, that last one must be a lie because here I am trying to figure this thing out.

In the midst of that morning's conversation the answer dawned on me. I may have thoughtlessly woken up the

Karma Fairy. In teaching my children about the laws of the Universe, that's the name I gave the force that causes what you send out to come back to you. The Karma Fairy is one of God's Teachers. She is ruthless in her desire for you to pay attention to your judgments about other people and about yourself.

For example, if you were to look at that man from your church who fell in love with the trapeze artist from the circus, and if you were to say something unwise like, "I can't understand how he could do something like that to himself and his family," the very next year you would find yourself in a mad affair with the mulch guy. You see unruly children in McDonalds and you sniff to your young self, "*My* children will never be allowed to act like *that.*" Ten years later, as you wipe barbecue sauce off your shirt and get your screaming child off the floor where she has thrown herself in a tantrum, you remember, and cringe. That's the work of the Karma Fairy

Here's how I attracted her attention. A tenth grader was interviewing me on the phone for a school assignment. One of the questions she asked was, "Have you ever had writer's block?" Listen. Can you hear it? Can you hear the dissonant chord of warning from the string section of the orchestra that plays background music to my life?

"No, I haven't had writer's block," I laughed, carelessly. "I have three part-time jobs and two children. I don't have time for writer's block." Diving back into work after hanging up, I didn't give it another thought. Until this morning, when it came to me that for the last four days I had been in school with the Karma Fairy.

I learned that writer's block doesn't have to mean you aren't capable of writing anything. For me, it means whatever I can think of to write bores me to slobber. Write about video poker? Boring. The rebel flag flying over the South Carolina statehouse? Boring. The trees they clearcut in front of my house? Boring. I know for a fact that these are emotionally loaded, interesting topics. The boredom is in me. Hello, writer's block. I found it doesn't take any extra time at all, and that I am vulnerable to it like everybody else.

Thank you, Karma Fairy. You love me, you tough old hag. You want me to be wise and kind, compassionate and careful. And you teach me over and over again this lesson I hate and cannot hold in my mind, that I am not an exception to any of the rules.

The Karma Fairy is here to show us that we are not safe in our righteousness, our intelligence, our careful nutrition, our common sense, our hip and groovy walk in the Tao. She is here to give us deep, full hearts. She is here to show us that we have it in us to make as big a mess as the next person. If we are ever going to find a cure for self-righteousness, the root of all separation, of all cruelty, we need her touch.

The stories in this book are all true. They are about her touch, about waking up, about feeling the Spirit wink at me, about living as a liberal black-belt minister mom in the South. It's an exotic life. I know yours is exotic in its way, and here is another thing I know: You have met the Karma Fairy too.

Where I Come From Is Like This

⌣

When I was twenty-three, I felt myself skating over the surface of my life. So focused on *who* I was, I wasn't paying attention to *where* I was. Beauties would pass me by. I would find my mind in tomorrow already, not noticing today. So I started seeing things out loud. "This is the time when the daffodils are blooming," I would say to myself. "The sky is pale blue, and there are wispy clouds way up high." My brain would retrieve the name of the clouds. Cirrus. My fifth-grade teacher, Mrs. Greiner, called them "horse tails."

One good part of my spiritual path is earth-based, so I like to know where north, south, east, and west are from where I sit. I like to know what is underneath me, too. Three hundred and seventy million years ago there was an ocean here in South Carolina. It was narrowing because the tectonic plate that carried the continent of Africa was headed this way on a collision course. Three hundred and sixty-three million years ago it plowed into the plate carrying the North American continent. The edge of Africa was pushed underneath North America, and it melted. The earth here was pushed up into mountains as high as the Himalayas. The piece of Africa that melted floated up to the surface as the granite along the Pacolet River, whose waters powered the textile mills where Spartanburg

County workers wove cotton into cloth until the mills closed down in the 1990s.

The rocks around my house were formed by heat and pressure eight to ten miles below the surface. They are on the surface now because, after the plates had collided for a hundred million years, they began pulling apart at the rate of an inch a year, eventually forming the Atlantic Ocean. Over time, weathering and erosion have removed maybe fifteen miles of surface. The Blue Ridge Mountains to the south and west of my house are the remnants of the towering peaks . . . not even the remnants; they are the roots of those peaks, having made their way up from deep below.

Under my house is dense clay soil formed by the weathering of the rocks that have come to the surface. They are crystalline rocks made up of crystals of quartz, feldspar and mica, pyroxene, amphibole, and olivine. As water seeps into the molecules of the minerals and mixes with acid from the roots of plants, these minerals change into clay. The quartz breaks down into tiny pieces and becomes sand.

My yard looks still, but it is not. Change happens fast and change happens slowly, but change is always happening. Geologists call that "dynamic equilibrium." The earth is on the boil.

Life, says Zen therapist David K. Reynolds, is "playing ball on running water." Dynamic equilibrium. In order to keep my feet under me, I have to remember where I am. I want to know the names of the trees and the grasses. It is my goal to know always, no matter where I am, whether the moon is new or full, waxing or waning. There is a sliver of a new moon today. It rose just after the sun rose and will set just after the sun sets. It will rise a little later every day until, at full moon, it will rise as the sun sets.

I have to know where I am in order to be here for my life. I don't want to skate along the surface. Getting oriented helps me dig in. So I talk to myself about what I see, about what the earth is doing, about where I am in time, and about where I am on the crust of the planet. What is it like where you come from?

Sandcastles

The other day I remembered a blue plastic bucket that was part of a mold for a sandcastle. In my mind's eye I could see the bright blue of it against the sand. At the Jersey shore, in the summer of '65, my dad and I would build sandcastles together.

Building the sandcastles was one of the only times my dad and I didn't talk. We were seldom quiet. There was almost always a back and forth flow between us. It wasn't exactly conversation. He would ask me what I thought of something. I would say a few things, then ask him what he thought. I suspected his questions were a way to give him space to think aloud, with me as his audience. I was his best audience. To be fair, he was mine too. Whatever I said was brilliant to him. I felt interesting and smart—as long as I turned it back over to him fast. I don't know, from here, whether that was his need or mine.

A green and a yellow mold had come with the blue one. The green was the straight part of a castle wall, and the yellow was a corner. We shoveled the wet sand into the blue bucket and patted it down with our hands. The sun roasted our pale Scots-Irish skin. Turn it over just right, lift the mold straight up, and you had a perfect castle tower with crenelations along the top . I loved the crenelations. I wanted to walk along a life-sized castle wall in a warm evening wind, looking out through the gaps, a scarf floating from the top of my cone-shaped hat, my dragonfly green dress shimmering in the dusky light. My quiver of arrows would be ready at hand, along with my bow in case of the sudden appearance of enemies.

These days the tide has washed thousands of times over what my father and I built together—over our conversations, over the morals and the religion and the politics. The clean and clear lines have washed away, but essential shapes remain. They affect my inner flow, not as much as they once did, but what my father gave me is still discernable. Does the fact that I've changed most of what he gave me mean that he failed? Not at all. The process of building with him—the pleasure, the companionship, the burn—is what shaped me. Building my own castles now with my children, I keep in mind that they are not forever. This feels like love.

The Lady Belches

The other weekend my boys and I spent the evening in a pasture around a campfire with five or six other families. Supper was over, and the kids were chasing each other in and out of the firelight. Suddenly a belch ripped through the air. All of the moms turned around. "That sounded just like my son!" one of us said. "Your son does that too?" we all asked each other. We each had thought ours were the only children who burped so shamelessly.

"What is it about the male digestive system that makes them have to *do* that?" one woman asked.

"*Some* of them do it on purpose," another claimed.

I should have kept quiet. I never do. I said, "My mother used to win all the belching contests when we were camping." A hush fell.

"Your mother . . .?"

"She was a great burper, what can I say?" I continued.

A friend was there who knew way too much about me. "*You* win all the burping contests at your house, don't you? I mean, aren't you the one who stunned your sons one night by being able to say 'Oh Boy' in one burp?"

It was dark, so she couldn't see the look I was giving her. Is there a Zen koan: If looks could kill, can they kill in the dark?

My mother was part southern lady. When conversations went over the line at the supper table, she used to change the subject by asking, "Does travel broaden you?" I managed to change the subject at the campfire without having to admit anything, but my friend was right. It is a tradition in my family for the women to be good burpers. Of course, we would *never* do it at the dinner table. One belched only in special circumstances like camping. Or driving, or watching TV.

As I said, my mother was a lady. She admired Queen Elizabeth and collected silver tea spoons from many nations. She could also ride a bike, put up a tent, and catch a beetle, and she lettered in track at her school in the Himalaya mountains. She used to let spiders live inside the storm windows of our house so we could watch the babies hatch out of their egg sacs in the spring.

Her religious beliefs were strong and conventional for the most part, but I remember a conversation about kissing when I was fourteen. I was holding forth with the righteousness only a teenager can muster. "Kissing really meant something," I said. "You have to like a boy a lot to kiss him, and you should make sure he likes you too. My mother looked at me, astonished, and said, "Meggie, don't you ever just kiss for fun?" She would sometimes touch the top button of my blouse and say, "Open another button, Honey, you look like you're choking."

Southern lady training holds that being ditzy is cute, so Mama would get lost on familiar roads. My sister and I would have to help her find Mama's Pizzeria where we ate pepperoni with extra cheese once a month, but every summer she would pack the two of us into the VW camper and take off. We camped in California, around Scandinavia, across Europe, and back again with her at the wheel. She made sure we saw the museums and cathedrals; she taught us how to find a campground in any town, how to eat Indonesian food, and to know you are never really lost as long as you have plenty of gas and you know what country you're in.

Back at the campfire, we sang, told stories, and had belching contests. Mama always won. Real ladies know when to take a break from ladyhood. I wonder who wins the belching contests around Queen Elizabeth's campfire?

The Point

◡⸬

I don't remember pizza in my early childhood. We were in North Carolina, living with my mother and her parents, since she and my dad were separated. I remember corn bread, fatback, greens, and vinegar. Those were from the cafeteria of the Mulberry Street Elementary School in Statesville. At home I remember scotch broth soup, green beans, and bologna. I remember that bologna didn't taste good at all when I ate it after I had brushed my teeth for the night. Nothing tastes worse after toothpaste than bologna, except orange juice. Once in a while my grand-parents would take my sister and me out to eat barbecue. Linoleum booths and a jukebox, along with the rarity of going out, made that a celebration.

Pizza became part of my life when I was ten years old. Mama and my sister and I moved back to the Northeast again so my parents could try being married again after three years of separation. My dad lived in Philadelphia, where they have great pizza. The best was at Mama's Pizzeria. A lot of times, Daddy would meet us there. On one wall of the place was a big cooler, and we were allowed to pick out our own sodas from the layers of cold cans. I always got Mountain Dew. The cans were so cold that one time a chunk of ice floating in the drink blocked the hole in the can and soda blurted out and got on my blouse. It wasn't a big deal. My parents didn't get upset about a little thing like that. In fact, we all laughed together. It felt tender. I loved seeing Mama and Daddy laughing at the same time.

In the summers Mama used to rent a two-story brown shingle house in Avalon, New Jersey. After a day of sun-bathing and sailing the Sunfish around the bay, she would drive us up to Ocean City and we'd walk the boardwalk. It smelled like creosote, salt water taffy, fudge, and pizza. At Mack and Manco's the guys would throw the circle of dough into the air and catch it, still spinning, over and over, until it was thin and flat enough to put into a metal pan.

I heard at school that you could tell where someone was from by how they eat pizza. Philly people fold it length-wise before they eat it. New York people don't fold it. They hold it above their mouth, tilting their head. If you use a knife and fork, you are from someplace no one even wants to know about. A girl in my tenth-grade class told me it was bad luck to eat the point first. I ate a bite of crust first for a while after that, but then I rebelled and recklessly began to bite the point off first every time.

I understand a lot more now about what my mom and dad were trying to do for my sister and me, trying to make their marriage work. They couldn't manage it. Nei-ther could I, as it turns out. My two boys travel between Mom's house and Dad's house, half time at each. They get to stay at the same school and keep the same friends. They eat pizza at a couple of different places. At one of those, even here in South Carolina, the guy tosses the dough in the air and catches it, keeping it spinning. It must be hard not to hold on too tightly. I imagine it takes practice to let the motion of the spin show you when to hold on and when to let go.

Maybe I didn't try hard enough not to break the circle of my parents' patterns. It is harder than I can say to have balanced my pain against my children's pain. I forgive my parents their confusion, their effort, and their longing now with a prayer that my children will forgive me. I am not ashamed of what I have chosen. I will be able to tell them that any time. I did the best I knew how to do. That's the whole point. That's what I have to bite into first.

My Bear Who Loved Me

⤳

I had a bride doll when I was a girl, and a teddy bear. My bride doll got married sometimes, but usually she danced with me. She liked to fly into danger and save her friends from bad guys. I brushed her hair and practiced braiding it. I dressed and undressed her, enjoying the feel of her white satin bride dress in my hands. I lost her shoes first, then the bottom tier of her dress. Her hair lost its curl, but her eyelashes stayed long and thick. I loved her. She liked me okay. I'm not sure why I didn't feel love from her. I think it had something to do with her being so much more perfect and beautiful than I was.

The one who really loved me was my bear. My father bought him for me six weeks before I was born. I carried him everywhere holding onto his left ear, which always hung by a thread. Bear slept beside me every night; I cried into his fur when I got sent to my room. He wasn't busy like my doll. Most of the day his ear was clutched in my fist, and he was adoring me. He didn't fall apart until I was thirty-two years old. I buried him in my backyard under a big water oak.

They say you get what you pay for. Aikido master Wendy Palmer says, in *The Intuitive Body,* that when you pay attention to something, you get the energy of that thing. Paying attention to a thing gives it power. If you pay attention to negative things, your life is filled with the energy of negative things. If you pay attention to positive things, you fill up with the energy of the positives. If you pay attention to your body, your body responds with better balance and grace.

When you pay attention to an object, you invest it with energy and love, and you increase its ability to affect you. I had a deep connection to my doll, and a deeper one to my bear. They were my treasures, not because they were worth money, but because attention had been paid. Love and energy were invested. Love came back to me.

I have a neighbor who is investing love and attention in a wooden pool chair with an orange and yellow striped cushion. One sunny day he was in front of his apartment sanding the frame of this chair while I was painting bookcases in the grass. Talking briefly, as neighbors do, we found that we had recent separation in common.

"This here chair was my favorite sittin' chair up at the house," he said to me as we worked in the winter sun. "We had a pool up there and I'd push the chairs into a little shed we had to keep 'em outa the weather. Well, things were getting bad, and what with one thing and another, this one didn't get put away. It was out in the rain all the fall and winter long, and you know what kinda rain we had. Well, this here is solid wood, and wood can't take being out in the rain like that. I thought about it a couple of times, but then I figured what the heck. Everything else was falling apart too. Why bother with it? Well now," he said, "I'm going to try to get it back. If I can just sand all this junk off the frame here and rub some vegetable oil in it, let it soak in good, it might come back. It's worth a try."

I am careless with most things. I nap in my clothes, I leave tools out in the weather, towels mildew in the washer, papers pile up. My belongings eye me with suspicion. Now and then I will have a fit of orderliness, and I beat back the chaos, but I think my things wish they belonged to people who, with calm mindfulness, polish and sweep and sort and mow and wash, rather than flinging things here and there to fare as best they can. I stink at mindfulness. I have to be motivated by love, and right now I resist loving things.

My treasures are my children, my lover, my church. They aren't as simple as my bear. I have given my heart to people I can't carry with me everywhere I go, and that feels risky. Loving my things would be safer than this. So far I'm choosing the risky path, though, and love is returning to me strong and deep. I'm getting big hugs and laughing afternoons and arguments and teaching times and challenges and frights and worries and pride and uncertainty and, now and then, I get to dance or fly around and save my friends from the bad guys.

Joy in Ordinary Time

⌣∴

My mama was a second-grade teacher at the Gladwyne
Elementary School in the rich suburbs of Philadelphia.
She loved the children, but she was shy with the parents,
who were financiers, pro ball players and attorneys, and
members of the Junior League, cricket clubs, and fox-
hunting clubs. For Christmas she would get amazing presents. One year she got a bottle of Joy perfume, then $150
an ounce. I don't know that she ever wore it. She was
keeping it for a special occasion. She kept it so long that it
finally evaporated.

With other things she was more openhanded. We had
grandfather's china and silver, which she often used.
"That's what they are meant for, to be used," she said.
"There is no sense in saving them. You'd never see them
at all that way."

That openhandedness didn't extend to her own person.
She wore sensible clothes, comfortable shoes, and white
cotton underwear. She had grown up the child of missionaries, and, whether she wanted it or not, that missionary
stream ran deep in her. She looked respectable and kind.
She was cute and cheerful and funny.

Joy perfume didn't fit who she seemed to me to be. A
daughter never does see all of the sides of her mother. It
makes me smile now to think that Mama harbored a hope

that an occasion would come in which she might walk into a room smelling rich and sophisticated, cherished and valued, in which it would be just the thing for her to wear. She let my sister and me smell it whenever we wanted to. The bottle sat like an honored but intimidating guest on her dresser. Whenever we smelled it, we marveled at how much it had cost.

I don't remember it ever occurring to me to wear it.

I want to let this lesson sink deep into me. Celebrate the body, the trooper of a body that carries you through life, that pleasures you and lets you dance. Celebrate your body now, before you have lost the weight, before you get your muscle definition, before you feel justified by the harsh eyes of your expectations.

Celebrate being alive, drawing breath, celebrate that you are achingly sad today and that it will pass. It is good to be able to feel feelings. Celebrate that there was a love so big and good that it hurt to lose it. That there was a time so sweet that you ache, remembering it. Honor the flowering of the tomato plants, the opening of the day lilies, the lemon smell of magnolias. Honor the ache of your heart and the tears falling. Life is mostly ordinary time. Ordinary time shot through with light and pain and love. Lavish joy on ordinary time. Hope is a wonderful thing. It is good to imagine a time when things will be better, but not if it makes you put off splashing yourself with Joy.

Deep Mysteries Have No Words

⌣

Yesterday I was writing a note of condolence to a mother and father who had lost a son. It isn't possible for me to imagine what they are feeling. It's hard to know what to say.

I sat with lots of people as a chaplain intern at Walter Reed Army Hospital. I talked to those who were dying, and I talked to their families. Our supervisors told us what not to say: "He's better off now" doesn't help, and neither does "I know exactly how you feel." You don't. "God took him" makes people mad at God. The supervisors kept telling us that our being there was what was important. "Yes, but what do we say while we be there?" we would ask.

"It's not about saying," they would answer like Zen masters. "It's about being there."

"But what does a chaplain do?" we would wail.

"You're the chaplain. What you do is what a chaplain does."

It was a mystery. We held hands with the dying, with the living. The thing that seemed to feel best was asking questions about the one they had lost. "What kind of person was she? Tell me about her."

I learned a lot that summer. It helped me some, early in the next year, in the dark of winter, when I sat with my mother as she was dying. "You're acting so normal," she said, barely audible. I hope she was glad of that. It was hard. Most of us withdraw from people who are dying. They seem to be in a different place, a jumping-off place to somewhere we can't follow. It is hard for us to stand with them at that place. Keeping them company is a difficult gift to give.

I don't know what the place is like that they jump off to, but I believe they're bound for somewhere. When we would call Mama's name, she'd whisper, "Just a second, I'll be right back." When her grandfather was dying, the family story describes all of his children and grandchildren gathered on the wide front porch. Through the open windows they heard him from his bed: "Jeremiah, I am James L. Pressly, from Statesville, North Carolina. Isaiah, I am James L. Pressly, from Statesville, North Carolina."

That story has stayed in mind with some power through the years. I am afraid of the process of dying, but not of death itself. That lack of fear feels like a gift. I am grateful to have been given that gift through family stories and sturdy beliefs.

It was awful to lose my mother. It was hard for other people to know what to do, how to be with us. People said all the normal dumb things, all the normal nice things too. It was all right, most of the time. Everybody meant well.

Being with a person who has just lost someone to death is standing in a place of pain and mystery. It is a place where almost all words sound pale and silly. The year my mama died, I was in seminary, surrounded by budding ministers who were eager to try out their pastoral skills. My roommate finally had to bar the door to keep me from being counseled to death.

What helped the most was being surrounded by a crowd of people talking normally among themselves about inconsequential things. That's what worked for me. Everybody's different.

I'm not sure what to write to my friends who lost their son. But at least I'm not feeling like there's one perfect thing to say hovering just out of reach. My note will be inadequate. It will sound silly. Deep mysteries mock words. That's why we have poetry and sacred scriptures. We keep trying to figure out a way to speak to each other about life and God and love and death and other unfathomables. I'll keep trying, if you will.

Night of Blood and Fire

⁓

My father was coming to visit for the first time in fourteen years. He had met my older son ten years ago in Philadelphia. He had seen my eleven-year-old only as an infant. It would take a book to tell all of the reasons for the distance between us. It is enough to say that I was seized up with dread and going in circles strategizing about how to handle it. My son, now fourteen, is going north to school. He will be an hour from my father, and I am determined that my son will not be hurt by his grandfather's lack of family skills. My father and his wife and their two children, the ages of my two children, were coming for a short visit. One afternoon, one supper.

I wanted to prepare the food ahead of time, so the night before the visit I put two pork tenderloins on the grill. In fifteen minutes I went out to check on them. They looked great, and I turned them. As I got back into the house, my friend Patt Rocks called and reminded me that her cable show I'd been on as a guest was airing right then. I had been promoting my new CD, *July Blue,* and talking to her about my new adventures as a singer/songwriter. "We're darling!" she said. I turned it on. "We *are* darling," I said. "You are more darling than I am, but not by much!" I watched it for the next half hour. When it was over, I was smiling, feeling happy. Until I remembered the grill.

I bolted out to the carport and saw the smoke. It smelled like tires burning at a landfill. I pulled up the lid and flames shot up as high as my head. The handles to turn off the gas were nearly too hot to touch. After the gas was off, the flames kept licking higher. The sides of the grill were on fire. I ran to the kitchen and grabbed a ceramic jug with a broken handle that was waiting on the counter to be fixed. I filled it with water and ran back out to douse the flames. When the smoke cleared, I saw the charred remains of the next night's supper. As I turned to go back in the house, the pitcher slipped and smashed on the concrete floor. The broken handle gashed the knuckle of my little finger, which began bleeding heavily. At the sink, washing the blood off, I looked up and saw that blood had somehow splattered the wall and the cabinets. I went to sit on the sofa. I was *not* having a good evening.

Telling my friend Pat Jobe about it the next day, he said, "You had Passover! You made animal sacrifices and splashed blood on the wall of your home, keeping the Angel of Death from killing your firstborn son."

As it turned out, the visit went miraculously well. My father was charming and sweet, his wife was dear, and their children were great. My sons got to meet their grandfather on their home turf, and he got to see the fine human beings they are. I got to sing for them, and they loved the songs I'd written. For the first time I didn't have to worry about my dad's feelings being hurt by my work, and he didn't feel like he had to register his disagreement and discomfort. I had done lots of work over the past years letting go of my anger and pain about him. Maybe all that work had done some good. Maybe he has been working too. It felt like a healing time, our one afternoon, our one supper. The Angel of Death didn't come to bother any of us. Was it the therapy? Was it the prayers? Was it the sacrifice of meat and the spilling of blood? Some things we may never know.

Kite Mother

In my garage there was a tired kite leaning against a wall. More than tired—it looked depressed. It was blue with a white dove in the foreground flying over a rainbow. In the 1970s it served as a wall hanging. I was in the low-budget decorating stage in which record album covers decorated the walls and my only table was a large wooden spool. When I got to the next decorating stage, in which I had Da Vinci and Van Gogh prints on the walls and an actual table at which to eat meals, I put the kite in the garage. It had never flown.

I had a vague picture of flying it one day with my children. The picture was lit with gold, and it had blurry edges. It was a greeting card view of motherhood, in which you have small children but you're not tired or irritable and you have energy for educational and stimulating activities. The sun shines on these motherly activities but it's not hot, and there are no bugs—unless you and the children are on a bug catching expedition. Then there are colorful, friendly bugs waiting to be caught and examined with calm delight.

Now, years later, I have actual children. We have a neighbor we called the kite doctor. He can make a kite out of a red bandana, a shopping bag, a bed sheet, or a Styrofoam plate. He built a two-inch square kite that his elderly mother flew at the Spoleto Festival Kite Contest in Charleston. The sticks were made of broom straws he had split in half, then split again and sanded. She flew the tiny thing from her wheelchair and won first prize in the smallest kite event. My boys cornered the kite doctor at our house one day and asked him to fix the kite in the garage.

He spent the next forty minutes, cheerfully and with good grace, sewing, stringing, and testing the kite. During the test runs he would call out to my six-year-old son, "Run now! Let it go! Stop. Run now . . ." The kite looped wildly, ignorant of how to fly.

Finally, the kite doctor decided to attach a longer tail. He unhooked some six-foot rainbow streamers that were fluttering from our front porch and attached them to the kite. When my son ran with the kite wearing its new tail, it took to the sky. My spirits rose with it. My children were having a perfect day, a day like the ones I had pictured when being a mother was still an abstract idea.

After the kite doctor went home, the kite was hung back up in the garage. It didn't look depressed anymore. My children wanted to fly it again after a week or so, but I realized a terrible thing. I am not a kite-flying mom. I love the idea of flying kites with my children, and it was wonderful that one day, but I don't want to do it again and again.

I keep hoping that tomorrow I will wake up and be the mother from the greeting card picture who has sweetness and creativity and sits for hours with her children making models of Indian villages and building a real canoe that we take down the Amazon together as we save the rain forest. I will wake up and want to bake fresh bread and serve fresh vegetables at every meal and fly kites with my children.

Some days I reach that ideal. We go on great hikes sometimes, and I like to draw with them. Maybe tomorrow we can draw a picture of the kite doctor and his mother sitting by the sea with the wind in her hair. She will be flying a two-inch kite from her wheelchair. In the picture it will be perfect weather, and there might be a large colorful bug sitting on one of the wheels of the chair. You know what, though? Into that lovely perfect picture my six-year-old son will probably draw flaming bombs dropping from the lady's tiny kite. I will laugh and clap for him. He and his brother are not blurry and golden. They are sharp and tangy and real. That's the kind of mother I want to be. Yeah, that'll fly.

Excuse Me, Was That a Conversation?

Sometimes I actually understand my children when we talk. Other times I don't. Each individual word they are using is familiar, but after the whole sentence has come out, I'm lost. My dream is to have actual conversations with them, and for them to be able to converse with each other. This is where they were a few years ago, at five and eight:

"I know lots of tricks in life on how to get candy."

"I invented them, not you."

"Uh-uh, Einstein did."

"How do you know that?"

"Einstein invented almost everything."

"Oh yeah? He didn't invent any of the good stuff. Like TV."

"Well, he didn't invent TV, but he invented electricity, and you can't have TV without electricity."

I couldn't figure out how to join in that discussion.

Now my boys are older. They play video games. The ten-year-old plays Pokemon cards. The thirteen-year-old plays Magic cards. They say things to me like this: "Mom, see, you combine the Splinter card with the Wagon of Mortality and you can replicate any number of freezes you want to. You throw them at your opponent and unless he has Reap the Whirlwind, you can deal him fourteen damage for every artifact you have in play."

I like it very much when they talk to me, even if, right now, it's talking *at* me. I remind myself that I'm grateful they like to do it. What I don't want is for them to turn into silent hulking teenagers grunting at me as they pass me in the hall. That will make me angry and hurt my feelings. Then I will lecture, which does not do any good.

My favorite times are when we have actual conversations, which are rare. Conversation happens when you say a brief thing to me and then I say a brief thing to you that has to do with what you just said to me. I may ask a question to clarify for me what you said, or one that asks you to go into greater depth. I may connect what you said to something else in my experience, but I try not to jump right to my experience. We can talk about yours first.

The art of conversation is a difficult one. Many people lecture or indulge in long explanations of their ideas or blow-by-blow descriptions of their golf game last Saturday. I was raised to do the "ladylike" thing in conversation with a man. Mama called it "drawing him out." The lady asks the man question after question so he can do all the talking. Finally I figured out that this is not conversation. I don't want my sons, when they are grown, to be comfortable with that kind of behavior, either from themselves or from their conversational partners.

My desire is eventually to have actual conversations with my children. Not a lecture from me, an argument about who is right and who is wrong, me "drawing them out," or a long-winded enthusing from them about whatever sport they are playing at the moment. We practice asking questions of one another. At the dinner table I will sometimes say, "Yes, you may be excused . . . after you ask everyone at the table two questions." They are getting better at it. It still feels sometimes like I'm tormenting them, but that's okay. I'm their mom. Tormenting them is my job.

Quitter

◡⋅

I wasn't raised with the pressure to stick with things that some of my friends were. They agonize over changing jobs or towns or ending a marriage, haunted by the voice of their dad or a coach saying "Don't be a quitter!" Don't get me wrong, I was taught that it is good to have persistence. My grandmother called it "stick-to-it-iveness." I gathered that you were supposed to use your judgment about what to stick to and what to let go.

I don't quit easily. I don't do it lightly or carelessly. I only do it when I'm no good for the job any more, when all the life is out of me. Often I make decisions by asking myself what I would want my children to do in that particular situation. Thinking about them helps me feel my way into what I want to model. If they are in a place, when they are grown, where they feel squeezed or suffocated, I want them to look at why they're there and what they can do to make the situation better. If there seems to be no way to make things better, I want them to have the option of getting out. I try to model for them when to persevere and when to quit.

They know from watching me that it's important to fulfill obligations. I go to work sick probably more than I should. I deliver speeches or teach classes even though, when the time comes, I ask myself why I ever said I would. I try to follow through with what I start. But when it's time to go, it's time to go. When your house is on fire, it's time to leave. When it's run or die, it's time to run. I think my sons will be able to smell the smoke.

Some organizations are like war. You are fighting on the front lines of a battle. I helped start a battered women's shelter in my town when I was twenty-six. I had lots of energy for it, lots of fight. I helped get it going, and I was president of the board for four years. Then I burned out. To a crisp. I couldn't stand to open the mail any more. It was making me sick. I quit. I didn't want to hear anything more about it. You can't have too many career soldiers in the heat of battle. You serve your term and go home. You let someone else take the work on. It's okay. There is a time to quit.

I was hearing from a friend the other day about the CEO of a large company who kept saying he was going to resign and go on to other things, but he couldn't let it go. He couldn't accept the way others were making decisions about the company. He stayed on too long. He got in the way. You can't keep doing things in a tried-and-true way forever. You have to change the way you do things, or you get stale. He was wanting to do things the time-tested stale way, and he was sucking the life out of the company. Finally, the rest of the board had to fire him, exclude him from everything.

It's sad when someone doesn't know when to quit. Even Jesus said there was a time to stop giving. If you go to a place and give your peace and blessing to that place and your peace does not return to you, shake the dust off your feet, he said, and go on your way.

I think there is a place and a time to be a quitter. Just because it's time to leave something doesn't mean it was never any good. Things have a life: a beginning, a middle, and an end. The end is the time to quit. Sometimes a situation is bad for you. That's when you know it's time to run out into the street and look for another place, or another way, to be, where you can be blessed, where you can be a blessing.

Night Prayers

Every night before bed, since my sons were little, we say the same prayer. We ask blessings on everyone in the family, then we say, "make us kind, strong, brave, joyful, useful, loving, honest, and healthy." In front of my eyes, at ten and thirteen, they are becoming young men I would choose as friends. I can't say how this is happening. Sometimes I think their father and I have a big influence over who they are turning out to be, and sometimes I think they were born strong individuals and our job is just to keep them safe and fed so they can grow up to be who they always were going to be anyway.

As is the way with all children, most of what they learn from me is nonverbal. Who I am and what I do has more impact than what I say. They will grow up to be a bit like me, a bit like their father, and a lot like themselves. They do listen to what I say. I know that because when they sigh at the start of a lecture, I can say, "Okay, you give me the lecture," and they do. I want them to know what I think and feel about things, and I think they do. I want them to know what I expect from them, what will make me feel like they are doing a good job. I have felt like a disappointment to my parents, and to God, and I have talked to a lot of other people who feel that way. When I ask, "What would have made your parents happy? What would *not* being a disappointment look like?" we're all stumped.

"I was just supposed to be perfect," one person said.

I decided I wanted my boys to know what their job description was, and nighttime prayers is a perfect time for putting it on the table. It was fun deciding what to put in there and what could be left out. I wanted it to be short enough so we could all remember it, with nothing in it that I wasn't willing to try to do myself.

Kind, strong, brave, joyful, useful, loving, and honest. Those were the first ones. Saying those things for about eight months, it began to dawn on me that we were leaving out the body. My spiritual path is one in which the body is sacred and important. Is "sacred and important" redundant? I must give that some thought. Anyway, I added "healthy" to the list.

Other things have been added over the years. As their dad and I divorced, we added my partner to our prayers, continuing to pray for their dad at my house, then, a couple of years later, for his new wife and her son and her parents, my boys' new grandparents. My dream is that we will begin to have an extended sense of family that includes ex-spouses and their new partners and their exes and parents. Some people are good at enlarging their hearts to include new people. Others are not so good at it.

We have not yet accomplished it in my family, but we pray as if it were already true. I had a wonderful talk with my ex-husband's new wife's mother last weekend at a basketball game as we were watching the boys play. She feels that families should be large like that too. "For the children," she said.

"Yes, Ma'am," I said. It's a good start.

Tea Evangelist

There is a gang of nine boys in our neighborhood. They flow from house to house up and down our cul-de-sac street. Usually at our house they play video games in which they fight robot mutants until either they or the robots get sliced up or exploded. Afterwards they slouch in front of the TV for fifteen minutes, still as zombies, their faces expressionless. Suddenly they move, with the coordination of a school of minnows, outside to the pines in the backyard where they climb to the very tops and sit in the patient branches, swaying in the wind and figuring out how to fall to the ground in ways that will look like the falling in movies.

When the horde of boys was at my house the other afternoon, my two sons were having a good time without me. This is good because it gives me a chance to write, which makes me happy. I cleared the dining room table, turned on the computer, and made a pot of Earl Grey tea.

As the tea was steeping on the counter, my six-year-old slammed in the door to get more darts for the Nerf blaster. The bergamot fragrance of the tea stopped him in his tracks.

"Mmmm, Mom, that smells good." He hovered over the pot, the neon green Nerf blaster gun swinging from one hand. "Can I have some?"

I debated reminding him about the difference between *can* and *may* but the last time I had asked his nine-year-old brother to tell me the difference, the boy had looked at me with exaggerated patience and said, "May is a month, and can is a metal container." I burst out laughing, and he lit up with delight at having made his mom really laugh. Since then I have lightened up about it a little.

So I said to my six-year-old hovering over the teapot, "Yes, you may have some," and I fixed him a mug with milk and sugar. He took a sip and looked up at me with stars in his eyes. Uh-oh, too much sugar. Another six-year-old slammed in at a full run, stopped on a dime when he saw his friend sipping tea, and asked if he could have some too. I put enough sugar in so he loved it too. Soon two nine-year-olds sauntered in and hinted that they might be persuaded to want some. Not that they were copying the little kids or anything. Within minutes all the boys but one were sitting around the table sipping sugary Earl Grey with milk. They pressured the last one to join them using the sophisticated technique of chanting "eight against one, we beat you!!" He couldn't hold out.

I'm not sure why it made me happy to see them all with their hands cupped around mugs of tea. I've considered the possibilities. Maybe I like introducing people to something new. Maybe my Victorian father, whom I carry in my head, was smiling and pointing out the civilizing influence of the female of the species on the male. Nah, that thought would have made me pour in dollops of Jack Daniel's.

Maybe I have evangelism in my genes. My father's father was a famous radio evangelist, and my mother's parents were missionaries in India for forty-five years. Granted, I was just making tea converts, but the satisfied feeling of souls won was disconcerting.

I feel a little guilty for converting a neighborhood of boys to Earl Grey tea by the calculated manipulation of sugar levels in their mugs. Does this make me as bad as the tobacco companies playing with nicotine levels to get people hooked on cigarettes?

It is a sweet feeling to share my pleasures. It was a delight to see a boy-gang take a break from an afternoon of robot slicing and falling out of trees by sitting around a table sipping Earl Grey in warm mugs. I tell my conscience to toughen up.

The Game Show from Hell

✦

I haven't said "What is this world coming to?" in a long
time. I feel things are going pretty well, on the whole.
Slavery is against the law in most nations, we have anes-
thetics for when we go to the dentist and antibiotics when
we have infections, and there is some good music on the
radio. It took me by surprise the other day, watching TV
with my children, to find myself horrified. I pride myself
on not being a crank, so let me tell you what happened
and see what you think.

We were watching an unfamiliar game show. The contest-
ant was shown photographs of three couples in silhouette.
She won a hundred dollars for each one she correctly
eliminated as *not* her parents. None of the three, as it
turned out, was her parents. Okay. Then she was offered a
trade: the three hundred dollars she had already won for
what was behind the mystery door (gasp!). Behind the
door were her sixty-something mom and dad, who had
been flown in from Texas to see her. How long had it
been since they had seen one another? Two years. "*Two
years* since she has seen them!" blared the game show host.
"Awwwww," said the audience. Mom and Dad were grinning shyly; they were on national TV. Their daughter,
who looked to be about thirty, was smiling back at them.
"Wait," said the host. Would she take five hundred dollars
and let the show put her parents right back on the plane

without a hug or a hello or anything? The mom and dad watched their daughter wrestle with this decision. She said, "n-o-o-o-o-o." She started to cross the studio to hug them.

"Wait," the host said. "Would you take a *thousand* dollars to put them back on the plane right now without a hello or a hug? "We-e-e-l-l. Yes," she said, and took the money! The audience was torn. Some cheered; some groaned. Her mom's mouth dropped open.

"Well, Mom and Dad, what d'you think?" asked the host.

"Well, at least she got the money," Dad said, trying to be proud of his girl.

"I'll come visit you!" she called, flapping the money in the air. The camera showed two old people walking slowly to the van that would cart them back to the airport.

I have complicated feelings about this. My mom died when I was twenty-three, and I haven't seen my dad in two years, maybe more. I have small children, and so does he, from the second family he started at the same time I started my family. We talk on the phone, but we live a twelve-hour drive apart. I know that all adults have complicated feelings about their parents. My boys will have them about me when they are grown. Still, if a game show flew your parents from far away to see you, most people would want to at least speak to them.

Even if you really truly would rather have a thousand dollars than a visit, would you want your parents to know that? Would you want the millions of people watching to know that? Emotional violence was done to those parents and their daughter by the show's producers. Emotional violence was done to the people in my living room watching such a brutal exchange.

I remember a science fiction book I read in high school that imagined us in the future watching televised surgery. A disreputable producer in search of a ratings boost offers a family free surgery for their ailing dad if they will allow it to be televised. They get extra money if they will allow the surgery to be done without anesthetic. Watching that game show, I remembered the science fiction story, feeling it had come true in front of me. How can a family recover from an experience like that? What did the show buy for a thousand dollars? What did they steal?

My boys and I got a chance to talk about families and money because of that show. We talked about what people do for money, what has been done throughout history for money. As usual I told too much and explained too long, and their eyes were glazed over before I felt finished.

I keep trying though. It's a crazy, beautiful, cruel, and loving world out there. In my family, I want us to aim for a balance of cunning and kindness. Our plan, should some sleazy game show host try to put us in that position, is to jump him and pound him until he begs for mercy. It's not the most socially constructive solution, but it satisfied the three of us that day. Maybe we could take up a collection for some prize money and offer the show's producers five hundred dollars each to apologize to the viewing audience. A thousand dollars to do it naked.

Treetop

Julia Hill has been living on a platform 180 feet up in an old-growth redwood for the past year, and she's not coming down yet. The tree was going to be cut by loggers, so Julia climbed up into its branches and stayed. She survived Northern California's winter of 1997–98. She thinks she can survive this one too.

I remember Church History 101, learning about men called "pillar saints." They were North African desert monks who lived on platforms high in the air in the early days of Christianity. Disciples provided support by raising buckets of food and water to the saints, who would live on their pillars for years. One writer described them as "dripping with vermin."

Julia Hill is twenty-four years old. The picture in *People* magazine shows that she is pretty; she has peace and humor in her face. Dressed in layers against the cold, she left her feet bare. In the photograph, one bare foot curves around a limb of the tree. I see her commitment in the way her foot shapes itself to the branch, connecting solidly to the live wood. I tore out the picture and taped it to the wall by my desk. I don't know why. I think I admire her. Maybe she's a saint. Maybe she's nuts.

It occurs to me that I don't have to decide. I can let myself simply be curious about her. She spends her time writing letters to supporters, reading what people bring to her. She talks to the media on her cell phone. I know she has visitors now and then. What does she miss from life on the ground? I would miss my children. I would miss movies, coffee with friends, restaurants, walking. Julia Hill eats vegetables and drinks rainwater. I want to know if she has given up sex. I want to know how she goes to the bathroom. Does she have lights or does she go to sleep when the sun goes down? She has tarps to keep off the rain. They make loud cracking and popping noises in the wind. I try to imagine what made her climb. Was it a spur-of-the-moment decision, or was it planned beforehand? I wonder if she cried those first few months at night, cold and wet and deafened by the noise of the wind and the tarps. I wonder how many times she has almost come down.

There are worse ways to spend a life than to become the champion of a great redwood. I know a good number of regular people who tell stories of a tree that sheltered and cradled them when they were children. I know people who, as adults, have felt an emotional bond with a tree. They draw strength and sustenance from their tree, and some tell wrenching stories of its loss.

One of the ways I figure out if something is worth my time and energy is to imagine myself on my deathbed. How would I feel, looking back on my life, about time spent on this thing or that one? Would I breathe deep in satisfaction and peace, or would I cringe in self-reproach?

If I were to look back on a year or more spent to save a tree, I believe it would make me smile.

I wonder how Julia Hill's mama and daddy feel about what she is doing. Her father is a minister in Jonesboro, Arkansas. Jonesboro is the town where two boys shot eight girls at their elementary school. The shootings happened a few months after Julia climbed 180 feet up and stayed. Her parents must have felt like the world was going crazy. It is going crazy—the world always has been going crazy. Still, you want your children to be normal. Holy people are not normal. The Gospels say Jesus's mother and brothers at one time thought he was crazy. Saints of every religion do outlandish things. Sometimes it takes a shock to wake people up from the sleepwalking life.

It would be hard to be the mother of a pillar saint. I would be wild with worry. Will she be safe? Can she be happy? What will life look like for her when she climbs down? Can she have a normal life? Will she be able to walk to the park and sit under the shade of tamer trees? Can she be part of a family when she comes down? Do you have to be a sleepwalker to live a regular life?

Will her spirit long for the treetop? How will her children feel, knowing their mother is capable of such extravagant acts? Will they fret that any morning they may wake up and look for her in her study, in the kitchen, in her bedroom, finally to find her singing to the sky, swaying back and forth in the branches of the tallest tree in the yard?

I know my wildness worries my children. My nine-year-old said, "Mom, please don't wear cowboy boots to my school when you read from your book to the fifth graders."

"Cowgirl boots," I answered absently, but I heard him.

"Mom, some of the kids think you're a little weird."

"How many kids, honey? Did they say something to you?"

"Well, nobody said anything. But I feel like some of them might think you're weird."

Poor baby.

What I know that my nine-year-old doesn't know yet is that even the soccer moms in their minivans have a streak of wildness. Scratch the surface and you will find it, even in women who wear bows in their hair and shoes with little heels. Any one of them would sit in a tree for a year if it meant the life of one of their children. Any one of them could shock you with what she would do if she and two friends were locked in a room with a child molester. Three quarters of them could describe seven violent acts they would like to carry out against their husband's TV chair and the channel changer he holds in the evenings. They could tell you about strong longings to sell everything and travel to Africa to feed hungry children, about passions burning deep inside for dangerous lovers, about things they have written that are hidden in their freezers under-neath the tops of wedding cakes.

We all hear the wind whistling through the treetops some nights.

Heart of Compassion

We were at Lake Blalock looking out over the water from a wrought iron table loaded with hot dogs and hamburgers, chips and dip. Sodas and beer chilled in tin tubs. My twelve-year-old was inside my friend Charlie's house playing pool. Three little kids were jumping off the dock into their mothers' arms. My fourteen-year-old was at the table with the grown-ups. In a few months he would go off to school in New Jersey, far away from this place.

My beloved friend Pat Jobe was across the table from me and my son was at the end of the table between us. "Boy, I got something important to ask you," Pat said, in an old man voice. My son smiled at him with half his attention. He had other thoughts in his head. He was spending lots of time with those thoughts these days.

"Now, boy, you listen to me here," Pat said, "This is something you goin' to remember for a long time, something you tell your children about, maybe even your grandchildren." Grinning, he grabbed the front of my son's shirt in his fist. He had the boy's attention now. Mine too.

"Have you got a heart of compassion?" My son wasn't sure he had heard right.

"Excuse me?" He was smiling, puzzled. Someone took a picture. I saw the flash out of the corner of my eye.

"A heart of compassion, boy, you heard me. Do you have a heart of compassion?"

"Uh—I think so."

"It's the most important thing, boy, more than hot cars and fast women, more than money or schoolin', to have a heart of compassion."

A week later we were standing in his new dorm room in New Jersey. It felt like it was a world away from our home in South Carolina. Dufflebags full of clothes and linens, a plastic basket of laundry supplies, golf clubs he had brought with him—everything was scattered on the bed, on the dresser, on the floor. He was going to grow into manhood far from home. "Do you want us to help you get all set up?" I asked.

"I think I want to go down to see my coach," he said, and stuffed his hands in his pockets.

"I guess we'll just get on the road," I said. "I have presents for you." I gave him a picture of all of us. Then I pulled out the picture of Pat Jobe leaning in close to him, his shirt bunched in Pat's fist. "Do you remember?"

"Heart of compassion," my son said with no hesitation whatsoever. When I visited several months later for Parents' Weekend, the picture was up on the dresser, the first thing you see when you come into the room. That boy's going to be okay.

The Terrible Weight of Good-bye

⌣:

Through one of the hardest weeks of my life, I was sustained by the hummingbirds at my window. It has been difficult, preparing all summer for my fourteen-year-old son to go away to school. It is something he wanted to do. There is a wider world out there, and he wanted to be out in it. I knew it was hard to get into the school he wanted to attend; I knew we didn't have the money. I didn't even let it be a real possibility until April, when he got accepted. In the same letter they told us he had been awarded a full scholarship. I wept, reading the letter. Then I started to try to get ready to let him go.

The last night my son spent in his room before leaving nearly undid me. The last bedtime prayers, the last "Time to wake up." The morning we were leaving on the long drive to New Jersey, I sat at the table in my kitchen and looked out at the garden. The sunflowers under the songbird feeder were bowing under the weight of their heads. The bird-eaten tomatoes hung forgotten on their vines. The garden dried up this summer. I couldn't make myself care. In working so hard to let my son go, I had let almost everything go. A hummingbird drifted up to the feeder and hung there, weightless. Another one buzzed by and they chased each other, then came back one at a time to hover in front of my window. Suddenly there was more air in the room. I could breathe deeply. My heart didn't hurt quite so much. I had never let that feeder run out, all summer long.

We got on the road that morning, and after eight hours we were in Pennsylvania. We found a steakhouse for our last supper together. I didn't cry. I had promised I wouldn't cry in front of him until I dropped him off at the school. When we got to the school, we took his things to the room and made the bed. I gave him pictures of us all together to hang on his wall.

"Well, I have lots to do," he said.

"Can we help you with it?"

"No, I can do it."

"So, you want us to hit the road, eh?" He nodded. He was ready. He wanted to go meet his football coach. This hardest part was lasting too long. We hugged. I cried. His little brother suddenly realized we were leaving him up there, and he broke down. We got in the car and drove out through the school gates. My younger son got over the worst of his grief by the time we got to Philadelphia. I still cry now and then.

My son loves his new school. Things seem fine. Inside I'm still screaming in panic that my boy is so far away from me. The hummingbirds are still a daily necessity. Their flight eases the terrible weight of good-bye. What will I do when they go?

Be like a bird, that halting in her flight alights
    Awhile on boughs too slight.
Feels them give way beneath her, and yet sings,
    Knowing that she hath wings

—Victor Hugo

Tonight You're Mine

✌

"Tonight you're mine completely." The song drifted out from us in concentric circles, a ripple in the dark air of the plane. It was near midnight and 130 of us were on an Air India flight to Bangkok. After a month of traveling together, we were weary and saturated with the rich sights of Israel, Turkey, Italy, and India. The purpose of the two-month tour was to study one another's religions. We were gathered from the four corners of the world, from a hundred nations.

"You give your love so sweetly . . ." The man who had started the song was a professor at UCLA. He was one of the instructors on this trip. Older than the rest of us, handsome, sophisticated, cool, he mostly hung out with the beautiful winner of the Miss India pageant or the languid and gorgeous Swedish grad student, neither of whose names I can now recall.

The plane was dark. Its engines hummed softly. Early that morning we had been in boats on the holy river Ganges. It is said that if you bathe in that river, you will be able to avoid rebirth into the world of suffering. Bodies of the dead are wrapped and set afloat on the river. All the sewers along the river empty into its waters, which are said to retain a miraculous purity. It looked filthy to me. This young professor had bathed in it fully clothed, dodging the sewage and the corpses. Coming up out of the water, his face looked enraptured. After cleaning up, he had been quiet for the rest of the day.

Most of the people on the plane were dozing or talking quietly. Some stood in the aisles. I heard him start singing, and I joined in with a harmony. When he heard me, he stood up, and so did I. Leaning against the seats, we sang across the border into Thailand, across the Asian midnight. I wanted it to go on forever. When the song was finished, I made my mistake.

"Maybe we can do that for the talent show next week!" I said.

I wish I could say he looked at me wisely and silently, teaching me about letting the moment be what it was, about being fully present with joy and then letting it go. He did not. He looked at me like I was the biggest geek he had ever seen, and he sat back down.

It was all right, though. I had been washed in the holy river of song. So there was a little crap that floated by. I could let it pass. I came up from under the waters, into the dark cabin of the airplane, humming along with the music in my head. I heard the Spirit say, "Will you still love me tomorrow?" You bet. You bet.

Trucker Angel

Driving the three-hour drive home from Atlanta, I was on
Interstate 85 when the traffic jammed up. We inched
along for a mile with no end to it in sight. I got off at an
unfamiliar exit. It was 11:30 at night. I stopped at a gas
station and went in to use the ladies' room, dragging my
map in there with me since I'm too old anymore to read it
by the light in my car. I couldn't see how to get around
the stuck place in the highway. Coming out of the stall,
I saw a slender woman in hot pants and a tank top with a
face that was on its way to looking like one of those shriv-
eled apple faces at a cheesy craft show. She had a tanning
bed tan. We smiled at each other.

She said it was hot, and I said yep it sure was hot. The
traffic was awful, I said, and I wished someone could tell
me a way around it. A voice called out from one of the
closed stalls, " I cin tell you how to get around it if you
like." Yes I would. I sure would, thank you. The second
woman came out and we washed out hands together, the
three of us. She was taller, and she had a Tasmanian Devil
tatooed on her leg. They were truckers. They had been
there a while, they said, since it takes a long time to gauge
18 tires. I didn't know what gauging tires was, and I didn't
know how to get around the highway construction, and
these two angels of mercy knew a lot about both of those
things.

The second woman said, "You take a right here and go till you see the Koo-boat-a on your left. Go on through that stop sign. "

"That ain't by the Exxon right there, is it?" the other one said.

"No, you're thinking of the other way; I'm taking her around the construction. You're crossing 8," she continued, "and you keep going across that and the road winds around and around and then you come out back at 85 north of all the construction, exit 11."

"No it ain't," said the woman with the tan, "that's exit 35."

"No, you're thinking of the other way. Go on," she said to me, making a shooing gesture with her hand. "Do what I said and you'll miss all this traffic."

I went the way she said to go. It didn't seem right at first, but I decided to trust her. Trust is hard for me. I figure that following someone's directions when the road seems to twist the wrong way at 11:30 at night in the middle of nowhere—that's trust. The amount of what I don't know is almost infinite. I can't control every minute of my life. Following a tatooed angel's excellent directions in the middle of the night is no spiritual leap into learning to trust, but it's a start, and I got home fine.

The Old Crone's Cauldron

I was struggling to straighten up with an armload of toys and dishes that had to go from the back seat of my old blue Honda into the women's shelter thrift store. That store is like the Old Crone's cauldron. Celtic mythology describes the Goddess's cauldron as the womb, the cook-pot, a place of death, transformation, rebirth. Visiting the thrift store, I put one thing in and pull out something else. I throw in clothes and games, baskets and pottery when they are finished at my house. I reach in and take out a black broomstick skirt, some brightly colored scarves, two square and heavy glasses from which my sweetheart and I drink gin and tonics when the weather turns warm.

A large woman carrying four shopping bags was watching my struggle from the sidewalk. Her skin was the color of coffee, no cream. Her hair was gathered into a tiny pony-tail that stuck out from underneath a brimless African hat.

"You a missionary?" she called to me.

"No, Ma'am."

"You got the look of a missionary," she said.

"I guess I need to wear more makeup."

"You got the Holy Ghost on you."

"Yes, Ma'am, I do," I said. It's been that way my whole life. I didn't want to get into it there on the sidewalk.

"Will you give me a ride to my brother house?" she asked, as I stepped up onto the sidewalk. "It's just there, down Magnolia Street."

"I'll be happy to," I said. "I'll be through here in a minute."

Harriet, who runs the thrift store, told me where to put the things and asked if that lady was trying to help me. She tried to help everybody, Harriet said.

"No, I'm just going to give her a ride down to her brother's house." Harriet nodded. She felt okay about it. That was a good sign. When the toys and the dishes were delivered, I held the passenger door open and the lady eased herself in.

Her directions were a little confused, and I had time, so we rode around for a while. She told me her name and I told her mine. She said I sure did have the look of the Holy Ghost on me. I told her I was a Unitarian Universalist minister. She asked where the church was, and I gave her directions. She promised to come sometime.

"I'd like to get together with you," she said. "We'll get together sometimes, maybe once a week. We could encourage each other, maybe be prayer partners."

"I already have way too many people wanting to get together with me," I said, "but I thank you." She took it pretty well.

"You buy me a fish sandwich right up there," she pointed to a dive by the railroad tracks.

"I can either drive you to your brother's house, or I can buy you a sandwich. I don't have time to do both." She took that pretty well too. We rode on toward her brother's house. Finally she motioned me over into a Burger King parking lot.

"Just leave me at this Church's Chicken right here," she said. I gave her the rest of the money I had with me, which was a missionary-ish amount, maybe three dollars, and watched her disappear into the restaurant.

The missionary thing stuck in my craw. Half my family on both sides have walked a missionary path. My mother grew up in India where her parents preached in dusty villages. I have cousins in China and some who grew up in what used to be Zaire. Being told I look like a missionary makes me want to wear five-inch red spike heels, black lipstick, and snake bracelets up my arms.

I talked about it with a friend who, with appalling insight, told me I had in fact been a missionary for years. My strong belief that the female face of God is vital, and my talking about that in speeches, classes, sermons, cocktail parties, and workshops, made me a missionary, she said.

Saying out loud, whenever I get a chance, that people do not go to hell made me a missionary, she said. Especially here in the South where hell haunts the deep layers of even the most liberated minds.

The word *missionary* had been tossed into the cauldron of conversation and had come out transformed. I'm walking that missionary path like so many in my family before me, with what feels like truly good news this time. John Murray, the first Universalist preacher in the United States, said, "Go out into the highways and by-ways. Give the people something of your new vision. You may possess a small light, but uncover it, let it shine, use it in order to bring more light and understanding to the hearts and minds of men and women. Give them not hell, but hope and courage; preach the kindness and everlasting love of God." Oh yeah, the Holy Ghost is on me. It's been like that my whole life. I hope the Goddess made it to her brother's house.

The Little Witch's Hat

On a cold night before Halloween, a new moon was rising over the chainlink fence of the baseball diamond. A thin crescent with its points turned upward, it was the moon the Babylonians called "The Horns of Isis." My children call it "Fingernail Moon."

After my son's ball game, I folded my canvas chair, wrestled it into its bag, and walked over to wait as the team ate a snack and the coach gave his final talk for the night. As parents milled around, I noticed a little girl dressed in pink holding her mama's hand. Her pink tights had big white polka dots. She looked about five years old, and she was wearing a black witch's hat.

Around here the conservative churches have nearly erased Halloween. We have Fall Festivals, or Harvest Festivals. The children "fish" for candy, dangling a string with a bent pin on it behind a curtain. A junior high school kid is behind the curtain, hooking candy onto the pins as they dangle. They toss bean bags through a hole in a piece of plywood and get candy. You get the picture. It's fun, and it's wonderful to watch the older kids have fun with the little ones, but it's not Halloween.

Halloween, according to Celtic tradition, is the time when the veil between this world and the world of spirit is thin. Ghosts haunt the crossroads; spirits play tricks. The dead come to visit. You dress like a goblin, like a witch, like a ghost because that's what you're scared of. You try on the idea of being tricky. You try on being scary. If you can act scary enough, maybe you won't have to be scared. If you acknowledge the fearsome trickiness inside yourself, you won't have to keep seeing it and fearing it all around you.

I was delighted to see that this little girl's mama let her have a witch hat. I must have been grinning at her because she let go of her mother's hand and spun around and around, making her way to me. She stopped in front of me and looked up. "I like your cowgirl hat," she said.

"I like your witch hat."

"I know spells," she said.

"A girl can't have too many spells," I said.

She spun back to her mother. I took a breath and looked at the moon. It has been hard, these last ten years, being a person who worships in paganish ways, singing at full moons and solstices, dancing in circles with friends, stamping my feet on the blessed earth in joy and gratitude for the spirit of life that flows through me and everything I love. I have felt lonely. I have felt foolish. I have felt fearful. I have felt passionately filled with God. In these times, I am surrounded by folks who are fearful of what I love. I can still smell the smoke of the fires that burned hundreds of thousands of women and men who were accused of being witches.

As the little witch and her mother passed me on their way out, she put out her fingers and brushed them across my leg. I looked down at her. She stopped for an instant, looked back over her shoulder at me with an almost grandmotherly expression of compassion and tenderness, and said, "Oh, my dear . . ."

Unblinking Witness

On the carport side of my house are two blue spots. The rest of the house is deep purple-gray. The spots mark the place where my ladder rested while I was doing the last bit of painting. I told myself I would let the paint dry and then take care of the spots. It has been a year and a half. I know the paint is dry by now, but I have some resistance to finishing. I want to figure out why this is.

Finishing would be depressing. I would then have to start on scraping, sanding, and painting the trim. When one job is finished, it is time for the next job. Maybe not finishing is a way of resting. That's part of it. I have no resistance to finishing writing jobs. I finish sermons and songs with ease. Cleaning jobs, now those I don't like to finish. I like leaving one dish still in the sink or out on the counter. It feels like a lie to pretend to finish a job like that. We all know dishwashing, cleaning, painting, any kind of maintenance is *never* finished.

Why not just make peace with the fact that I am fighting chaos constantly? Why do people pretend that they finish things like that? Why not leave a little chaos on purpose so I can let the Universe know I get the joke? That way I can feel I have some control in the unfinished nature of the situation. Yeah, that's it.

I remember looking at myself in the mirror, brushing my teeth. I must have been twelve or thirteen. It struck me that I was going to have to brush my teeth at least once a day until I died. Thousands of times. I was outraged.

The two spots of blue on my house feel like a rebellion. They say, "I know this job isn't finished, and it's never going to be. Raking leaves, brushing teeth, washing dishes, they have to be done over and over. Finishing is an illusion, and I know it. You haven't fooled me into acting as if I'm through, even for a minute."

Maybe I have to learn my steps in the dance of ongoing process. I talk a good game about letting go of control, acknowledging that the journey is the teacher, not the goal. But the two blue spots on the side of my house are a mute and unblinking witness to the fact that I still fight. I want to be able to do all the housework my house will ever need and then never do it again. I would love to do a week of constant exercise and never have to do it again.

I can think of ongoing processes I love: writing, eating, talking, making love, gardening, watching movies, reading. I don't have any outrage about not being able to do at one time all the eating I will ever need to do. Thinking about making all the love I will ever need at one time just makes me laugh.

Can I learn to love the process of cleaning? Can I learn to think of painting as a pleasant pastime? It looks like too much of a stretch right now. I'm going to leave that resist-ant, rebellious part of myself unfinished too. I'm going to leave few a unpainted, unimproved spots on my character. To match my house.

Baking with a Bad Attitude

I had not baked bread in a long time. I used to be good at it. I used to make my own yogurt, for heaven's sakes. Within the past year I had actually been thrown out of one friend's kitchen. Not for bad behavior, of course. For incompetence.

For my women's spirituality group we were each to bake a loaf of bread, kneading into it our gladness and delight. French bread used to be my favorite, so I decided to try. It had been years since I had seen the recipe that came with my long loaf pans, so I got out *Joy of Cooking*. The French bread recipe had impossibly cheerful notes accompanying it. These people actually enjoy cooking. I shuddered.

I had to cook supper at the same time I was putting the bread together, so the yeast had to wait. I did not have time to coddle it along. The scalded milk got too hot, then I added the yeast, sending up a quick wish that the heat didn't kill the yeast. It foamed sweetly and started smelling just like—well—yeast.

I was dumping the flour into the bowl—instructions were to sift it, but everything is presifted these days, I was pretty sure. Suddenly remembering I hadn't melted the shortening to go into the milk and yeast mixture, I melted some butter and swished it around in the cup to cool it down so it didn't kill the yeast. I had forgotten the sugar too. I added sugar and then the still-too-hot butter, then went out to turn the dinner steaks on the grill. I washed lettuce, then sat the kids down to dinner. I realized there was no way to put bread-making on hold while we ate supper. I slapped my fork down and let my supper get cold while I added the milk, yeast, and butter to the flour and stirred. My spoon hung up in a layered, caked mess. Hmmm. Maybe I had been a little too reckless in measuring the flour. There wasn't enough wet stuff to make the dry stuff look like it was supposed to look. It had to rise, so I put it in the warm oven to rise for two hours.

At the end of that two hours, close to my bedtime, the loaf didn't seem to have gotten bigger. Maybe when I kneaded it, it would get all soft and elastic like it was supposed to. I was sleepy. I read the recipe again. No kneading was called for. When was I going to let my damn gladness and peace flow through my hands into the stuff? I shaped it into loaves and got ready to shove them into the oven so I could go to bed. I read the directions one more time. Have I mentioned I don't follow directions well? I found out the loaves now had to rise again until double in size. They looked scabby and cracked. Maybe as they rose they would get smooth and lovely. I stuck them on the dryer so they would rise faster and lay down to doze. After another hour they were still ugly. I was too sleepy to care. I put them in the oven to bake. My drooping eyes reread the damnably cheerful, picky little directions about letting them bake for fifteen minutes at one temperature, then turning it down. I did what they said to do, but without a really good attitude. When the baking time was nearly done, I turned the oven off without giving the loaves a glance, and went to bed.

The bread, in the morning, was heavy, hard, hideous. There is some spiritual lesson here. Mindfulness? Attention? I don't know. I don't have time to think about it.

Home and Garden Overload

.·:

I knew I was in trouble when I found myself flipping on the TV as I passed through the room just to see what Norm was making in his New Yankee Workshop. Oooh, he was using his miter saw. I sat down to watch. My breathing became deep and regular. All the little things that had been occupying my mind just drifted away as I watched shavings curl away from his router. He talked so calmly as he worked, and he always reminded me to use safety glasses when I did any woodworking. That was a motherly touch. Nothing could go wrong with my life if I were as calm and thorough as Norm. Even his name is— Norm. The Norm. I imagined his finances, his home life, his driving, calm and perfect. Measuring twice, cutting once, confident and productive.

Norm was the beginning of my addiction to the Home and Garden Channel. As my addiction progressed, I moved on to other shows. Next was a woman named Beverly who can fix a dishwasher or install lighting in a corner cabinet without even chipping the dusty rose of her polished nails. The gardening shows are fascinating and beautiful. I'm in love with my garden, so I love hearing about massing zinnias, naturalizing tulips, mixing potash and nitrogen, or something like that. There was the House Doctor, who knows how to take a brick facade apart with an air-powered chisel so you can fix water damage in the wall behind the brick. There were perky women and men who, with varying degrees of taste, redecorate rooms. I started counting how many times they used the word *nice*. These redecorators seem to divide themselves into the cozy camp and the open-and-airy camp. The cozy ones call the open-and-airy look "cold," and the ones who like things open and airy call the cozy rooms "cluttered." I think they just redo the same rooms over and over, making what is cool and airy cozy again, then turning what is cozy and cluttered back to cool and airy. I come down definitely on the airy minimalist side, myself.

I am a big fan of a wild, skinny Englishwoman who saws holes in closet doors; builds Hindu temples in people's gardens; and paints walls turquoise, purple, and green. I'm not sure I would turn her loose in my house, but I want to follow her around and cheer her on as she swoops into someone else's place and transforms it without a flicker of hesitation. I can do my therapy practice like that, but I leave my closet doors alone.

At first I rationalized my addiction. I could control it. The only effect on my life was that I now had a vase full of grasses from my backyard in the dining room and a row of chairs hanging from hooks in my carport. Oh, and I'm painting my house purple. But that's all.

I realized I was in over my head the other day when I heard myself talking about getting a frame from the flea market, some fabric and some batting and covering the frame, maybe making a stamp out of a raw potato, dipping it in gold paint, maybe putting stars all over the fabric. My blood ran cold. A little Norm for meditative purposes was one thing, but batting?

I remember batting. I bought some once when I got an urge to do some quilting. Some friend told me it was easy. It took me a week and a half to make one square of a pattern called Dinner Plate. It was in rose and blue, which tells you we were in the early '80s. I get surly when I work with my hands, and I was *not* easy to live with for the duration of the project. I'm not going there again. No batting. No way.

Maybe I can keep my addiction in check. I think I can give up the shows about antiques and knickknacks. I can avoid actual woodworking. I would probably make crooked tables and stairs that lead to the wrong place.

It is deeply meditative for me, an intuitive word person, to see these people working with their hands. Peace of mind comes from watching people who are coolly competent in an area that is mysterious to me, where they stand so clear, so solid and unambiguous. What doesn't make sense to me is perfectly understandable to them. That is deeply reassuring. I'm not giving up Norm.

I Learned Not to Hope

✎

I learned not to hope God would heal cancer. I watched my mother hope God would heal hers. She found a lump in her breast when she was forty-five. First she tried not to think about it. I'm sure she prayed. The lump didn't go away. She waited a year to go to the doctor. He performed a mastectomy and gave her radiation, then performed another mastectomy. Mama was in and out of the hospital for the next five years. Over and over, we heard the cancer was gone, that God had healed her! We rejoiced. Over and over the cancer came back.

She went to faith healers. They were not kind or intelligent people. Several said she wasn't healed because there was an "unconfessed sin" in her life. My mother, a saintly woman, searched her soul for what the unconfessed sin might be. It infuriated me that she was loving a god, believing in a god who would sit in heaven with arms crossed, telling her, "I could heal you if I wanted to, but I'm not going to do it because you have an unconfessed sin in your life. I'm not even going to help you a little bit by telling you what that sin is."

Sometimes in conversation with my mother it was as if I tripped the switch on a tape recorder and out would come Morality Talk Number 43 or Religion Talk Number 17. A singsong tone in her voice would betray that a canned speech from the deep recesses of her childhood had begun. An Avoid the Appearance of Evil tape ran when I wanted to go camping with my boyfriend in eleventh grade, which was closely related to the What Will the Neighbors Think? speech my friends' mothers gave. I know I have canned speeches I give to my boys too. I just don't know what they are. We are all blind to our own blind spots. I'm sure when they are teens, they will let me know. I think those speeches come when you are talking about something you're not sure of in your core. You think you ought to be sure, and you want your kids to be sure, so you give them the speech that was given to you. It's not an honest thing to do.

Mama was exceptionally honest in most things. Once we left a drive-in movie, drove around, and paid a second time, because she had paid the under-twelve price for my sister, who had just turned twelve. I came home from school one day to find her crying at the kitchen table. She was feeling ashamed because a postcard had come for me and she had read it.

Her cancer made her honest about the rest. Once her own mother gave her some advice and she disagreed. My grandmother muttered, martyred, under her breath, "How sharper then a serpent's tooth is an ungrateful child." Mama spoke sharply to her mother for the first time and said, "Mother, I am *not* your child. I am forty-six years old."

When she was telling me this story, she teared up and said, "Meggie, I know I have treated you like a child, and you're not one, and I apologize." Well, I was about twenty-one, and I thought I *wasn't* a child at that point, so I said something gracious like. "Oh, Mom, you've never really done that . . . . But she wasn't finished. She said, "If I had it all to do over again, I believe I'd say no to you less when you were little. We said no, no to you all the time."

She never did tell the truth about dying. Her faith won out over experience and common sense. I don't know if that made it easier for her. I hope it did. It was not easier for me. She didn't talk about dying until right at the end. She called me at seminary and said, "I think the Lord is taking me." A kind student drove me the hour and a half home, and I got to sleep by her sofa through that last night. She died the next morning early. We never said good-bye.

Zen Bowling

I had been bowling maybe four times in my life when I took my children bowling three weeks ago. I wanted to play too, not just sit like the smarter parents, watching the children play. It was a character-building experience from start to finish, from getting the bowling shoes all the way to seeing the final score. I purely despise character-building experiences.

First, let me tell you about the shoes. As a woman, you have to talk encouragingly to yourself often when your feet are bigger than Clementine's number nines. Mine are. The sweet boy behind the counter had to give me shoes in a men's size because they didn't have a women's size big enough to fit me.

I'm strong, so I picked out a ball that weighed thirteen pounds. I thought it might knock over more pins. When my turn came, I pulled my arm back and brought it forward, imitating the people who looked like they knew what they were doing. When the moment came for the ball to go flying toward the pins, everything went into slow motion. The ball was still attached to my hand. Finally, the ball came off my thumb with a loud *pop!* It dropped into the gutter and rolled slowly away. My thumb hurt.

With a lighter ball and a larger thumb-hole I could conquer this. After a quick check with my boys to see if they were too embarrassed to stay at the bowling alley with me, I tried to follow their instructions about what to do. "Aim for the middle pin," my younger son said, "Well, not the exact middle, over to the side of the middle pin." "Point your foot in the direction you want the ball to go," said my friend Kim. "Let the palm of your hand face the pins." Elbow turned in, feet pointed forward, body loose, I flung the ball toward the pins. It clipped the corner pin and knocked it down.

Okay, I said to myself. Loosen up. Let Beginner's Mind take over. We'll do Zen bowling. Don't think about it too much. Just roll the ball toward the pins and let it happen. Three more pins fell. My older son was playing almost as badly as I was. I suspect he was doing it to make me feel better. He hit the corner pin and it toppled. "Yea!" he cheered, sarcastically, "I knocked down another one!" My younger son wandered toward the line and dropped his ball with a thunk. It rolled casually toward the middle pin, hit it solidly, and all the pins fell over.

I was still working on Beginner's Mind. Let go. Think about bowling *through* the pins. In karate we hit through the target. In karate I can do it. Bowling through the pins, I think I knocked over four.

Loosen up your body. Don't think. Gutter ball. Enough of Zen Bowling. Let's try really really hard to do everything right. I knocked over two pins.

I hate being this bad at something. Maybe it can be a spiritually deepening experience. Maybe I should try to embrace my incompetence, get comfortable with being this bad at something. I'm good at a lot of things, I said calmly to myself; I don't have to be good at everything. I can learn to be bad at this. I can enjoy it anyway. Curses! Becoming more spiritual wasn't making me any better at bowling either. Back to Zen mind. Let go of outcomes. Breathe. I am unattached to whether I knock pins over. I am being in the moment, bonding with my boys, laughing. I still secretly wanted to bowl better. Being unattached to outcomes was just another sneaky trick to try to do well. This Zen stuff is more complicated than it first appears.

This time, in the second to the last frame, I said to myself, "It's time to do well." I have said this to myself before. Four pins fell over, then two more. It was the last frame. I flung the ball straight toward the pins. It was a beautiful sight! Time went into slow motion again. The ball flew fast down the center of the lane and struck the center pin on its side. All the pins scattered. It was loud. What a great sound! I didn't remember how I did it, but here was another turn, and I wanted to do it again. What was different? I had been wanting this all along. I flung the ball again and got another strike. Two in a row, right at the end! What's my score now? Sixty-four? That's not too bad. Is it?

A Very Dead Bird

ᠵ

You know how road kill can stay on the road so long sometimes, it becomes completely flat and dried out? That is how the bird was on the asphalt in front of where I was standing at the Confederate Memorial Day ceremony. It looked like it might have once been a pigeon.

I had three boys with me. We were on our way up I-85 to hike the King's Mountain Battlefield Trail, a battlefield from the Revolutionary War. Two of the boys were mine, seven and ten, and one was a neighbor, eight. They too were fascinated by the very very dead bird in front of my feet, more so than by the soldiers in period costume with their muskets and powder horns, their gray hats and mustaches. A weeping Confederate widow was there in black bombazine hoop skirts. She wore black lace gloves and had a black parasol to keep the sun off her white, white skin. The woman who had invited us to this ceremony played the widow's friend, supporting her by holding onto her elbow. She was a Civil War reenactor from California, where they didn't much care if they were assigned to play Union or Rebel soldiers. In South Carolina, she mused, they *care*.

A tall white politician was speaking at the microphone, which was not working. We could only hear every third word or so. He was rocking onto his toes and bouncing for emphasis. The speech needed some *emphasis.* He was droning on about pride . . . the many dead . . . noble suffering . . . the heritage of our great state. Nothing, of course, about scars in dark skin, babies sold away from their mothers, New England families rich with slave trade money. That bird was dead. So dead.

It seems to me that the more we retell a story, the more it loses its original shape. We run over and over it so many times, trying to remember, trying to feel the same things we felt at first. We leave out the complicating parts, the parts where we don't look heroic. Soon we can barely make out what the reality of it used to be. The life in it changes, goes flat. Divorced people drone out the list of wrongs and bitterness, leaving out the complicating facts. After twenty years of doing couples counseling, I know this: What seems very simple when you've only heard from one partner suddenly becomes hugely more complex when the other partner takes a turn to talk. Winners of wars paint the enemy as demonic, less than human, deserving what was done to them. Losers of wars tell stories of noble innocence and suffering. All of the stories are true in some way, but the bones and blood are gone. They've been run over so many times there's no real life in them anymore. I stared at the very dead bird wondering what was to be done about all that.

Suddenly the soldiers were loading their rifles, and they shot a loud volley into the air. My older son yelled, "I didn't do it!"

That's what they all say.

Message from a Large Prophet

⸎

I was sitting in a prayer meeting in Jerusalem in February of the year I was twenty. The couple I was living with was there, a Swiss woman who was married to an American man. A young soldier in the Israeli army named Steve sat next to me. There were others at the prayer meeting, but these are the ones I remember. A large American lady was in attendance too. She didn't believe women should wear pants or cut their hair, and she felt God spoke to her directly about his plans for other people's lives.

We had been praying a long time when this large lady stood up and said, "Thus sayeth the Lord: Meg should marry Steve," and sat down. I opened my eyes and looked at Steve, who was looking back at me with unflattering alarm. It was an awkward social situation, one I have never seen covered in a book of etiquette.

It is also an awkward theological situation, when someone tells you what God wants you to do. Fortunately, my father had thought to warn me about this very thing. He said, "If God has something in mind for you, he will tell you about it, so if any guy tries to tell you that it is God's will for you two to get together, tell him you'll wait for God to tell you about it." My dad was a man-hater. He told me all men were rats, that there was no end to the tricks they'd pull.

My father's father had been an evangelist on the radio, a great one for telling people what God's will was for their lives. He guided his four children with a firm grip well into their adulthood. He used to joke that his wife and children sometimes got him mixed up with God. Then he would chuckle, as if that were not such a bad thing.

I think it's a terrible thing. Letting someone play God in your life is called idolatry. When we get a preacher or a husband or wife or a parent mixed up with God, something is wrong. If they seem to enjoy being mixed up with God, run the other way as hard and fast as you can.

The awkward moment at the prayer meeting in Jerusalem came and would have passed, only Sylvia and Ted, the couple I was living with, had themselves gotten married because of a similar message from God. They had met in Holland. Sylvia had been meditating and praying some weeks after they met and said she had a vision of Ted's face and heard a voice telling her this was the man she was to marry. She went to him and told him he was to marry her. He was deeply troubled. He was not in love with her. Furthermore, he argued, since he was the man, God should have come and told him instead of telling her, since the man was to be the head of the household. That put a damper on things until an evangelist from India came to town and told the story of a woman who came up to him after a service and said God had told her that she was to be his wife. He married the woman. Ted was persuaded.

When I knew them, they had been married four years and had three children. Sylvia had also heard God tell her that he didn't want her to use birth control, and they were living a cranky and exhausted life.

Hearing the voice of God and falling in love have a lot in common. It's hard to tell when or where or how it's going to come, and you can't make it happen. Nobody can do it for you, but both hearing the voice of God and falling in love eventually happen to almost everybody. That night at the prayer meeting in Jerusalem, though, I don't think either one of them happened. Steve and I didn't fall in love, and I don't think that lady was hearing the voice of God. I know she wanted to, though, so if she's still trying, I hope it happens for her. I wish both hearing the voice of God and falling in love for her, and for all of us.

An American Story

ᴖ

It's 3:30 Sunday afternoon in Chesnee, South Carolina, and the cruisers are revving their engines. Every Sunday for the past fifteen years, this small town has been both backdrop and stage for an American drama. The players? Teens in cool cars, the police, and the preachers.

The cruisers ride along 221 from the elementary school to the high school and back again. "What are some of the things they do to make their cars amazing?" I ask six kids sitting in one car in the parking lot of Turner's restaurant. Chrome rims on the wheels, they say, lowering your car so it rides close to the pavement, tinted windows, neon underneath the frame so at night you look like you're floating. As long as the neon doesn't strobe. You get ticketed for that.

The kids feel mistreated and misunderstood, and they talk heatedly about the injustice of a new ordinance that requires them to clear all parking lots after 9:00 PM. A sturdy blonde boy says, "Some little punks, they vandalize and stuff, they throw eggs and toilet paper. Most of the kids just drive. No fighting, no getting high, no getting drunk." It does back up traffic, but what's the big deal? The cruisers say they buy gas and cigarettes and Cokes, and they don't hurt anybody. They certainly are not going to hell for cruising, like the preachers are shouting up on the sidewalk in front of the Lightning Lube 'N Lather. I make up my mind to go talk to the preachers later.

A police officer pulls up. Everybody freezes. Nothing stiff, just an indrawn breath, a stillness. He gets out of his car and asks three cars and a pickup to move off the sidewalk. He gets back in his car. This feels like part of the dance. The kids are seeing where the limits are, testing how far the rules will bend. The officer has the answer.

It's time to visit the preachers. Seven white men and one woman are standing in dress clothes on the sidewalk in front of the Lube 'N Lather. During the week you get your oil changed and your car washed there. Sunday afternoon it's a place for cleansing and renewal of the soul. The woman is holding an umbrella for shade. One fresh-faced preacher is pacing back and forth with a Bible in his hand. He is shouting, and his voice is getting hoarse. They all smile at me as I come toward them. When I say I want to ask a few questions about their preaching to the cruisers, they point to their pastor, an older man in a suit and tie, hat, and mirror sunglasses. He is standing to one side, behind a fellow holding a big American flag.

As we talk, I can see my reflection in his glasses. "Some of the kids think you're preaching that they're going to hell because they cruise, but I couldn't believe that was true," I say.

"That's a lie," he says. "There's nothing wrong with riding up and down." Why do they preach to people going by in cars—isn't that frustrating? They preach out here, he told me, because this is where the people are on Sunday afternoons. The men take turns preaching. I ask if the woman preaches, and he says no, she's here with her husband. I ask if anyone has ever been converted because of their preaching on this sidewalk, and he says he thinks maybe a few.

"There's only two places to go," he says, "and you're either going to heaven or hell. We hope people hear a few words and think about them later. We're not here to hurt anyone. We're here to help."

The police want to keep peace and order. The preachers want people not to go to hell. The kids just want to see each other; they want to test their power, their appeal, their freedom riding up and down between the high school and the elementary school, with the police on one hand and the preachers on the other. The school. The law. The church. The kids. How free can you be? The age-old drama is playing every Sunday afternoon in Chesnee, South Carolina. No charge for admission.

Mike's Mission

I was in my old blue car with my eight-year-old boy headed west on Reidville Road. I had just driven past two brown shoes lying on the median strip. One was turned on its side, but the other one was turned like it was headed to McDonald's. I was wondering about those shoes, how they had gotten there on the median, what their story was. Then I passed something that made me wonder in a different direction.

It was a tan and navy Chevy Silverado parked in a vacant lot. On either side of the truck bed were big homemade signs with stenciled letters, black on white. The sign I could see read, "MOM + DAD ARE YOUR CHILD-REN SAVED? THE DEVIL IS AFTER THEIR SOULS." I had seen this truck before, parked up in Chesnee, north of Spartanburg. A rangy white man had been sitting in the passenger side of the truck that day, and there he was again.

One of my hobbies is talking to people who aren't going with the flow. I wonder what makes these people paddle against prevailing currents. I turned into the vacant lot, parked in the shade, and told my red-headed son I was going to go talk to the man with the signs. He and our greyhound dog decided to stay in the car. Grabbing my pen and notepad, I headed for the pickup truck.

The rangy man was dozing when I walked up. He had on a white button-down shirt with its sleeves ripped off worn open over a white T-shirt and jeans. He found a look that suited him in 1963 and he stuck with it. My footsteps startled him awake. He saw me and gave me a sheepish grin. He had blue eyes in a weathered face, a sprinkling of gray hairs among the brown fringe of bangs that flipped up slightly off his forehead. His embarrassment was my first clue that he wasn't one of the ugly crackpots. The ugly ones would probably wake up afraid or mad.

"I've seen you a couple of times parked here and there, and I wanted to come ask you some questions," I said.

"Well, sure, that'd be all right."

"First let me write down what your signs say." The one on the other side of the truck said, "GOD HAS PROVIDED ONE WAY TO ESCAPE HELL AND JESUS IS THE ONLY WAY." On the front of the little sign-holding house he'd built on the back of the truck the stenciled letters just read, "ARE YOU SAVED?"

"Can you tell me why you do this? What kind of response you get? What kind of conversations you have with people because of these signs?" I ask too many questions all in a row. Ask my ex-husband.

"Well," he said, looking at me sideways, "It's actually kind of rare for someone to come talk to me." I realized he was wondering if I might be some kind of crackpot myself.

"I just think of myself as somebody who kind of prepares the ground so a seed can be sown. You know in the Book of Revelations it talks about the Great White Throne of Judgment, and God says there can't be no place found in Heaven for some people. And the Bible says preach the word, so that's what I'm doing. Trying to do what the Lord says do."

"Just plowing up the ground," I said.

"Yeah. I want to loosen up their hearts, to get them to thinking."

"How long have you been doing this?"

"Well, this is about the third summer I been out here. I'll do it 'til about the end of August, unless the Lord tells me different. I don't even live here in Spartanburg. I live about thirty miles away from here."

"I've seen you up in Chesnee."

"Yeah, I been in Shelby; Boiling Springs, North Carolina; Blacksburg, where I live; and Spartanburg. I been here since 7:15. Around 12:30 I'll go over to Westgate Mall area 'til about 2:30, then I'll go home. I was scared when I first started."

"What were you scared of? What was the fear?"

"Well, I had a guy threatened my life because he owned a liquor store and one of my first signs said, 'BUD,

COORS, JACK DANIEL'S IS OF THE DEVIL.' He didn't scare me off, though." He pointed to the word *devil* on the sign nearest him and said, "The fear? This guy."

"You're afraid of the devil?" I asked him, "You believe that there really is a devil who is after our children's souls, like your sign says?"

"The devil will kill," he started ticking off his points on three fingers, "and destroy . . ." I can't remember what the third thing was because I didn't write it down and this kind of thing won't stick in my head. "When he says 'kill,' what do you think he means?" the man continued. "We all going to die anyway, so what's he going to kill? Our souls, that's what."

He preached a little more, and I could tell you the gist of what he said, but most of you have heard it all before, and as I told you, that stuff doesn't stick in my brain. He would reach now and then for his gray leather Bible and hold it in his hand. I asked him what he thought about while he sat there. He didn't really answer me. He told me sometimes he stood by the truck and waved a little black Bible to get people's attention. He showed me the one in the glove compartment. He had worn it out waving it at cars for three summers.

I remember he talked about how people didn't have an idea about sin anymore. He said, for example, that homo-sexuals used to hide like roaches and scatter when someone turned on the light. Now they are right out in the open, he said. Funny how that did stick in my memory.

I asked him what his name was. He said it didn't matter. Jesus was the one he wanted to talk about. He told me that he had been saved in 1981 when he was twenty-nine. He'd been rough and wild before that.

"Drinking? Drugs? Running around? Violence?" I asked.

"Everything you can imagine," he answered.

He went back to the wild life in his mid-thirties, then got colon cancer. His colon exploded, is what I got from his hand gestures as he talked about it. He took treatment for about five months, he said, then he rededicated his life to the Lord. He figured the Lord was trying to either get his attention or move him to the graveyard. Never went back to the doctor until 1995, and the cancer was gone. "Mike's life was over," he said. "Mike didn't owe nothing to this world anymore. I died back then, is how I look at it. This here's another life for me. Not for Mike, but for Jesus."

I asked him if he didn't have trouble with a god who would get someone's attention by giving them cancer. I mean, would he get his daughter's attention that way? Was he a kinder dad than God? He shrugged and said, "Well, you know, I may be wrong, and you know how you can mislead yourself, but here's how I figure it . . . ."

He went on to explain how he figured it all, and it was interesting. For me, though, he had already come through. When I find a person like Mike who is doing something with passion, and who can also hold the thought in his head that he may be wrong or deluding himself, I celebrate.

Even toward the end when he asked if I were a Christian, it was okay. I told him I tried to follow the teachings of Jesus, but that was all. The way churches taught Christianity now, I said, wasn't very good for us women. I was glad it was working for him, though. He didn't drink or treat his wife badly anymore, and that was pretty good.

His wife was the greatest, he said. There wasn't a woman alive who should put up with what she had, but she'd stuck by him. He started telling me that the Bible said women should listen to men and raise children instead of work, but I could see the specter of his wife rise up behind him. He stopped halfway through a sentence, threw up his palms as if to ward her off, and said, "Of course, this is a different time, and women ain't gonna put up with that no more." He shook his head, laughing.

You know, it may be restful to see things as black and white as Mike does. "Right is right and wrong is wrong," he said, "like white is white and black is black." Here's my problem: Right is complicated, and so is wrong. If you know anything about color and light, you know that black is complicated, and so is white. It's a mysterious world when I can stop to talk to a religious nut and find myself liking the guy even though he compares members of my family to cockroaches. I listened for the fear, and it wasn't there. I listened for hate, and it wasn't there. Maybe I'm achieving a heart of compassion. Maybe I'm lazy and have no principles. I'll let you know when I figure it out.

Holy Cow!

My realtor was driving with both hands on the wheel, at ten o'clock and two o'clock. At first I thought she might be hard to talk to, but we were warming up to each other, telling stories. A colleague of hers had just helped the new rabbi in town find a place to live. He was a nice man, the woman reported. He had been a cantor for years before going to seminary, singing the ancient words and melodies for the worshippers in a synagogue on the West Coast. "Sing me something," her colleague had urged him. He had, and she said he sang like an angel. The woman told the rabbi that his voice was wonderful. Her daughter was getting married in a few months at the Presbyterian Church, and would he consider singing something at the wedding? The Lord's Prayer, maybe? My realtor giggled. He said he thought maybe his new congregation would not understand if their rabbi were to sing this most Christian of prayers, even though they all agreed Jesus was Jewish. My realtor looked sideways at me and smiled.

We live in such a small town. For most people, the only religion they know is Christianity. It is hard for them to step outside the well-worn paths. Did I say "hard for *them*" as if I weren't part of it? Pardon me. Let me tell a story about myself now.

When I was in my latest possible twenties, I traveled around the world with people from a hundred different countries. We were studying one another's religions for two months. My roommate for the two months of the trip was a Hindu woman from Sri Lanka named Mangalam Lakshmanan. She was tiny and cynical with an elegant British accent in which she could swear like a drill sergeant. As the alarm woke us for a 6:30 bus, she would roll over in bed and groan, "They are trying to kill us." One evening we heard one of our group pass by in the hall cussing up a storm in a bad British accent. She looked at me, outraged. "People with whom I am not even acquainted are trying to imitate me," she said.

One of her favorite ways to express disgust was to say "Jesus Christ!" After a couple of weeks, I asked her gently not to do that any more. "That is the name of someone who is sacred to me, and it feels funny hearing you use that name the way you do."

She was gracious about it, of course, and stopped immediately. Several weeks later we were talking late at night in the hotel room. She was telling me a story about her mother, who used to throw up her hands in frustration at Mangalam and say, "I must have been a very bad person in my last life to have been visited by a daughter like you in this one."

"Holy cow! Your mom said that?" I said. She stopped dead and put her hands on her hips.

"Oh?" she said with her eyebrow raised, "I cannot say 'Jesus Christ,' but you, in talking to a devout Hindu for whom cows are sacred, you can say this thing?" We collapsed, laughing. I'll bet the new rabbi would have laughed too.

Love, Not Fear, Is Spoken Here

It was around Christmas time, and I was horsing around in the kitchen with my first-grade son. I had a candy cane in my hand. "Mom, do you know what that candy cane makes when you turn it upside down? It's the letter *J*."

"So it is," I said.

"Do you know what the *J* stands for, Mom?" I was beginning to sense the way this conversation was going. We live in South Carolina. The letter *J* only stands for one thing.

"Jesus!" he crowed.

"Cool!" I said.

"And, Mom, do you know what the red is for?" Oh no. He doesn't go to a church that would go there with candy canes. Not with the children.

"What does the red stand for, Baby?"

"His blood. And the stripes?" *No.* "They stand for the stripes on his skin after they whipped him." This was *not* from church. Not at Christmas time.

"Honey, where did you hear this?"

"At school."

"Was it from your teacher?" For some reason, my teeth were clenching together.

"No, from Christopher's mom. She was at the Christmas party at school, and she gave out candy canes and told us this story."

I called the teacher, and she said she had been horrified, but she hadn't known how to stop the mother in mid-story. This wasn't the first time that strong odors of evangelical Churchianity had come wafting over to our house from the school. There was the teacher who sang at the end-of-the-year talent show about how Jesus helped her teaching. There was the second-grade boy who sang a song at the Christmas school show about how you had better be saved because soon it was all going to be over and if you didn't have Jesus, you'd be going to hell.

Another Christmas someone invited a puppeteer to come to a Christmas potluck at a Presbyterian church I used to go to. She came dressed in white robes, and she had a lilting singsong-y voice. If she had been blonde, she would have looked like Glinda, the Good Witch of the North. Her puppets were cute, and they told the kids to be honest and loving. At the end of the show, she came out from behind the puppet theater with an enormous book in her hand.

"Children, do you know what this book is?" she asked.

"The Bible?" answered the innocent and alert Presbyterian children.

"No," she said, "It's the Book of Life. If your name is written on *this* side," she gestured with one graceful hand, "You go to Heaven to live with Jesus. *But . . .*" I heard a scritch-scratching sound like a match being struck. *No.* The entire left side of the book burst into flames, and she held it there, burning without being consumed, some prop made for a children's show out of fire gel. "If your name is written on this side," her voice grew low and sorrowful, "you go to burn in hellfire forever."

The parents stood, frozen. She invited the children to come forward and kneel for a prayer for the salvation of their souls from hell. To their credit, the parents moved in with their children, arms around them, kneeling beside them for the duration of the prayer.

I like to think that if I had been the woman then that I am now, I would have done something. In the movie I play in my mind of how it should have been, the scene goes into slow motion as the page bursts into flames. I stride out of the crowd of parents toward her and see that three more parents are with me. One of them distracts the kids as I snatch the flaming prop from her hands and snap it shut, tossing it off into a corner of the room where it skids to a stop against the wall. Two others take her arms and walk her out the door into the December evening. The stars shine clear and bright in the silent night as we set the puppet gear down in the parking lot. We look up at the sky and breathe in the light. The children laugh inside the warm building. We must insist. Love, not fear, is spoken here. Love, not fear, is spoken here. Love, not fear, is spoken here.

Graffiti Education

I think the statute of limitations has run out on this crime, so I can now tell the story. I'm not the kind of person who takes the law into her own hands. Usually. But one church I drove past every day had been working on my nerves. This particular church is anti-abortion and anti-choice, and they had been making that plain. People, of course, have a right to their opinions, and we all have a right to express those opinions, as long as it doesn't harm anyone. I'm all for that.

I hate abortion, but I vote pro-choice. Abortion is a violent solution to the problem created by our culture's attitude toward women and babies. If we really loved babies and wanted them to be born, we would not attach so much shame to pregnancy outside of marriage. We might even see the babies as gifts rather than punishments for unwed sex. We might celebrate pregnancy and help young mothers raise their babies by providing child care in the schools and colleges, rearranging the way we do things to give young mothers and fathers a chance to participate in life while still being parents. I know, you're asking, "What planet is she living on?" I remember now. That's why I vote pro-choice.

As I said, this church is anti-abortion and anti-choice. The whole winter previous to this they had about a hundred small white crosses planted in their front yard. That's fine; they have a right to do that. It made me want to plant some crosses of my own—for women dying from illegal abortions, for children dying from abuse, for the crack- and nicotine-damaged children now staggering through our school systems, for the grandmothers struggling to raise children they did not bear.

I didn't put crosses in my yard, though. It would have been too hard to explain, and the well-meaning church people weren't hurting anyone. I could stay out of it. Until they took the tiny crosses down and in their place erected a large white sign.

The sign said, in big black letters: "PREGNANT? NEED HELP?" Then there was a black line under those two questions and under the line a phone number.

I thought to myself, what kind of help might they be offering? I knew they were well-meaning people, so surely they weren't the kind that would steer pregnant women in trouble to those places around here where they sit you down and show you pictures of fetuses mutilated by late-term abortions. They probably would put up the pregnant women in nice pro-life homes until they gave birth. Then the nice pro-life people would probably help the woman and her baby financially, not just until the birth, but until the child got to school, so mom could keep going to school or work to support herself and her child. What that church probably did was provide free child care for young women who chose not to have abortions! I was getting excited. After all, many church buildings are underused during the week, especially during the day, and there are sweet pro-life retired people who would watch these unaborted children and teach them how to read and share and get along with others. I decided that was the kind of help the sign was talking about. The sign didn't say all that very clearly, though. I decided to fix it.

Late one Saturday night a friend and I took a walk by the sign. I had white spray paint and a large black permanent marker. While she bent to tie her shoe, drawing the eye of any driver who happened by, I used the white spray paint to erase the black line. We walked a little more while that dried. Then we walked back and, in the blank space where the line used to be, I wrote in large block letters, "FREE CHILD CARE."

The sign now read "PREGNANT? NEED HELP? FREE CHILD CARE, then the number. Now that was more like what I was sure they meant. When I drove by Sunday morning before church, small clumps of people were looking at the sign. By Sunday afternoon the sign was gone, never to be seen again.

What Are They Promising Again?

∿

The newspaper in Spartanburg called me for a comment about the Promise Keepers rally. Reporters' guidelines say they have to get comments from male and female sources, racially diverse sources, pro and con sources. I was supposed to be the white female con source. Actually, the reporter was hoping I would be the rabid "Feminazi" source. Sometimes I rant and rave about things in public. I try to think it's part of my charm, but it unnerves some people.

I can't get too upset about the Promise Keepers—yet. I see large groups of men having spiritual experiences together. That can't be bad. Men are bonding without beer. Men are cheering and chanting without teams on the field. Men are looking at their lives, taking inventory, resolving to do better. They are loving one another, they are realizing their religion instructs them to love their brothers of other skin colors, and they are creating small groups of support for each other for their new lives of integrity. I respect spiritual experience. When people open their arms and laugh and weep, things start to move. What's to complain about?

Well, okay, there are just a few things. I applaud the resolve of these Christian men to live without cheating on their wives and abandoning their children. I get worried, though, when they talk about how the women in America have gotten out of hand. The Promise Keepers preachers spout the propaganda of the Radical Right, blaming the perceived breakdown of the culture on the "breakdown" of the family.

I see the family evolving into new shapes and forms. The old forms weren't working anymore. The "traditional" family the Right points to was concocted by businesses and advertisers after World War II, when Rosie the Riveter had to be shepherded back into the kitchen so the man coming home from the front could take her place on the production line. Suddenly we had Betty Crocker in an apron and pearls.

Psychology joined in, nipping at Rosie's heels to get her back into the kitchen. They churned out books about the awful consequences that followed missteps in mothering. Everything that went wrong with the children was Mom's fault. Mothers and children had to bond correctly or the kids would turn into psychopathic terrorists. Mothers should not coddle their sons or the boys would become homosexual. Mothers should not be too powerful or their sons would be homosexual. Mothers should not be too distant or their children would be insecure. Or was that if mothers were too close? I get confused. Fathers, this whole time, were ignored by psychologists as the cause of any of their children's ills. They were at work. When they were home, they watched TV. What harm could that do to the family?

Nowadays we healthy mothers are rolling our eyes when we are blamed for every glitch in our children's lives, and many of us are working outside the home, mostly because we have to. It takes two incomes to have a regular American life. Also, fathers sometimes don't stay in their chairs and bring home the paychecks. To their credit, the Promise Keepers seem to have noticed this, and they are resolving to be faithful providers for their stay-at-home wives so the traditional family can be recovered. Wonderful.

The part of that "traditional family" myth that scares me, though, is the part where the man has authority in the household. This is the concept that lights up the Promise Keepers crowd. They get this concept from the Bible. When most people hear the word *authority*, they think it means the power to make people do what you want them to do. This kind of authority has to be upheld either with violence or the threat of violence.

The Promise Keepers point out, quite correctly, that the Christian concept of authority is different. It comes from Jesus, who said men should have authority as servants in their families. That's great. So these Promise Keepers say they will come back from the rally and have authority in their families as servants. But I wonder: Do they have any models for that? No. Nowhere in the world is it shown to a man how to have authority as a servant. I hope this is what the Promise Keepers talk about in their small support groups. They accept the mandate of being the authority in their families with alarming enthusiasm and noble resolve. These men know how to quarterback. But a family is not a football team.

They accept the responsibility of being willing to give up their lives for their wives. They come back from the rallies and wash their wives' feet. Fine. But how many times in the daily life of a family is the man called on to die for his family or wash feet? I searched my experience for things they could do instead until that dying for your family thing comes up.

Instead of washing feet, let the Promise Keepers go wash in the laundry room and at the kitchen sink. Let them learn how to notice when the bathroom needs cleaning and do it without being asked, and without wanting applause and sex in exchange. Let them start dinner before their wives get home from work. Let them make the grocery list and go to the store. Let them help the children with homework.

I want men to come back from the Promise Keepers rally knowing about whites and colors, and I'm not talking about race relations; I'm talking about doing the wash. Let them come back from the Promise Keepers rally knowing how to sew on a button, hem their own pants, take time off from work to volunteer at the third-grade Halloween party, and stay the weekend by themselves with three children under seven.

Let them come back from the Promise Keepers rally knowing how to ask their wives how they're doing that day, who they talked to, what their hopes and fears are, and let them listen to the answers. With the TV off. If a man came back from a Promise Keepers rally knowing how to ask his wife three questions in a row about herself and her life and listen to the answers, his wife would faint from joy, he would get more sex, and I'd be a Promise Keepers fan.

More Sex, Less Anguish

꒰

I read about a couple who owns a video store and is making tons of money editing people's private copies of *Titanic*. Are they taking out the screaming? The despair? The death? No. They take out the two steamy scenes between Kate Winslet and Leonardo DiCaprio. People say they don't want their children watching sexual scenes.

I don't understand these people. I have two boys. Right now they are nine and twelve. I would a hundred times rather they watch kissing than shooting. I am distressed that they watched *Titanic* because they had to see women, children, and men die. They had to watch people be mean to each other. They had to watch screaming and crying. What horrors! I'm not upset that they saw a man and a woman appreciating each other's beauty, touching each other, loving, and kissing. What is the matter with people?

Why is it that on the Family Channel, you can watch shoot-'em-up after shoot-'em-up and never see a sexy movie? Why is killing more family oriented than kissing? Our culture seems to be more comfortable with violence, anger, and despair than with sex. You can watch torture in an R-rated movie, but you can't see a fully naked body.

Is sex so dirty? Is it more damaging to the psyches of young viewers? I think the Family Channel shows more death than sex because the Church has spent so much energy in recent history trying to keep kids from having sex before they are married. It has always made a place for killing. You apparently have to kill sometimes. People get out of control. There are bad guys, and you have to kill them. In war, there is the Enemy, and it is okay to kill the Enemy. It seems that there is something in the American psyche that sees something clean and curative about killing. We only really want to see bad guys get killed. Well, except for the good guy's family, at the beginning of the movie, to give him that good, clean rage he needs to motivate him to cut a swath through the Mafia or the gangs or the international cartel or the wicked government agency or whoever is going to get decimated this time. So the bad guys are okay to kill, and the good guy's family, and oh, of course, young, beautiful women. Those women are doomed on TV and in the movies. There is rarely a slasher chasing eighteen-year-old boys or middle-aged women. People seem to enjoy watching young and beautiful girls get slashed to pieces. The young girl can be doing something provocative alone, dancing around in lingerie and high heels (the way normal American women do when we are home alone), but by god don't make anyone watch a young and beautiful girl have her breast kissed. That is going too far. Sexy scenes with violence soon to follow—that's okay. Sexy scenes with no violence to follow need to be edited out of movies seen by impressionable young minds.

Even though I have told my children all along that I would rather they watched kissing than killing, it has barely sunk in. My youngest still says "eeeeeuuuwwww" when he sees people kissing. He can watch someone getting shot without batting an eye. If blood spurts, he might say, "cool."

Maybe it's a kid thing. Maybe it's a boy thing. I'm pretty sure the Family Channel is run by grown-ups though. I'm still trying to figure out their thing.

Floozy

"Don't let your cat be a floozy." The cartoon on the Humane Society billboard showed a female cat up on her hind legs on top of a fence, one paw behind her head, the other one on her hip. A crowd of tomcats crouch below, ogling her. My sons saw the billboard and asked me what a floozy was. They sensed it was something like a "slut," a word about which they had heard me shooting sparks. Here is how that conversation went.

"Is a slut always a girl?" I stamped my foot.

"Yeah, Mom."

"Is there a word your friends use for a boy who gives himself away too freely?"

"Player, whoredog, ummmm."

"Are those insults that people say with contempt, or is there usually an undertone of admiration in those?"

"Some admiration, I guess, Mom."

"*So.* I don't want you to use a word that is an insult that mostly is thrown at women unless you have an undertone of admiration in your voice when you use it. *Okay?*" Not exactly what I wanted to say, but there you go.

They asked, "so 'floozy' is like that?" It is, I said. I started trying to talk to them about the billboard, and now I'm confused.

What I know about female cats is that they go into heat. When they are in heat, they want to make babies. They want it really a lot. Tomcats want to make babies all the time. Tomcats will try to make babies with females whether or not the females are in heat. They don't need a female to strut back and forth on the fence showing her stuff. They don't need to be seduced or cajoled. There is no need to tempt a tomcat.

My father, the worst male-basher that ever lived, told me men were tomcats. "They are only after One Thing, Meggie," he would say, "and they will do whatever it takes to get it." We have all heard that men think about sex once every eight seconds, and that women don't think about it but once every ten minutes or so. Here is my confusion. If that is true, why don't men admire and love women who want sex and have sex easily? Why are women who have a lot of sex with different people treated with contempt? Why are there so many contemptuous words, purely sexual in nature, used for females and none that are commonly used for men that aren't spoken with that undertone of admiration?

And another thing—why are there articles on the cover of every women's magazine about how to turn men on if they are already always turned on, like tomcats? Why is nearly all sexy underwear for women to wear? Why are almost all the sexy movies for men? If women are supposed to be harder to turn on, why is there not merchandise all over the place to help men turn women on? Why do men not trade love-making techniques on the golf course? From what my male friends tell me, men exchange conquest stories, but technique is something you're already supposed to know. I feel for men. First, there is the pressure to be always wanting sex like a tomcat, and then the expectation that they are really good at it without ever being taught.

Maybe that's why, even though the belief is that women are slow to "warm up," there still aren't many articles in men's magazines about ways to seduce a woman, ways to make love so she will want to do it again and again. If great technique is not what turns women on, why not try to find out what *does* turn women on? Actually, I know the answer to that. Intimacy turns women on. Talk to her. Ask her questions and listen to the answers with eye contact and no TV on in the background. Remember something she said several days ago and quote it back to her. Remember some details of her life, notice things, ask her how she feels about things, let her talk about problems without trying to solve them for her. But if she had intimacy, then she would want sex, and that would make her a floozy, and that would be bad. Help me with this. I'm trying to explain it to my kids.

Smashing Things

✌

"Do you ever feel like smashing things?" I was taking a battery of psychological tests at a tiny desk at a career counseling center in Atlanta; this was question number 554. I answered yes. The purpose of the test was to indicate how sane I was. I had already answered hundreds of questions, from "Has someone been following you?" (No) to "Have your stools been black and tarry lately?" (No again). I know I'm sane. I don't worry about it. I told the truth on all of the questions because it's important to me to be honest. Also, I'm very bad at lying. I don't have the focus or the attention span to do it well.

The psychologist sat across from me calmly. We were having a conversation about my test results. "In the middle of a very normal-looking test, Meg, you answered yes to the question 'Do you ever feel like smashing things?' Can you tell me about that?" His voice was calm, neutral, alert. He was ready to explore this crack in my seemingly sunny disposition.

"I take karate," I said.

"Ah," he said.

I love karate class. I get to hit big pads and little pads and hanging bags. It makes me feel happy. I'm easy to live with after karate class. I have no road rage. I have patience with my children. Some people get inner peace through meditation. I get it by hitting things. Hard.

I have been in karate class for nearly six years now. I have a second-degree black belt. I don't think I could quit if I wanted to. When I have to sit out for a month because of an injury, I get restless. I miss the smell of effort, the sounds of impact. I miss the loud breath, the yells that energize my arms and my legs.

There is a bond among the adult students, especially those of us over thirty-five. We tease and gossip and cheer. Four of us got each other through the black belt test. It lasted five hours. We had to demonstrate everything we had ever learned. We punched and kicked and spun and jumped. After two hours I was exhausted. We divided into partners and sparred with each other.

Four hours in, I started thinking about how I would explain to my friends why I had to quit. I couldn't think of a way to explain it. We did katas, the formalized fighting patterns that are dances of power. My friend Joanna, standing next to me, was drawing on her last reserves. She looked at me and said, "We're all right." I said, "Yeah, we're all right." I couldn't quit because I couldn't leave her. Maybe she was thinking the same about me. Ten more minutes passed. "We're all right," I said to her. "Yeah," she panted.

After four and a half hours the teacher said it was time to do the fitness portion of the test. A hundred sit-ups, then a hundred push-ups. A hundred kicks while balancing on one leg. Then a hundred while balancing on the other leg. My body was crying. I tried to explain to my body why we were doing this. My brain wouldn't hold a thought. I wanted not to throw up. That became my biggest thought. Plans to finish the test faded. My ambition for accomplishment faded. All that was left was not wanting to have to tell the story of how I threw up and quit.

After the punches and the kicks, the sparring and the katas, the gasping and sweating and reeling, the sit-ups and the push-ups came the weapons. I have a long, slender wooden staff called a *bo*. In the weapons katas I get to whoosh it around my head and jab with it; I get to twirl it and spin with it. It is satisfyingly loud and impressive. Energy came from somewhere, and I did my kata with focus and power. When I finished, the moms and dads in the gallery burst into applause. I had forgotten they were there. It was a great moment. I managed to stay standing up while the belts were presented. I got to my car and shut the door before I started to sob. It was two weeks before I could talk about any of it without crying.

Yeah, I like smashing things. I smashed my ideas about what this forty-something body could do. I smashed my resistance to practicing. I smashed my self-hater who kept asking how I could stand up in front of those full-length mirrors week after week surrounded by whip-thin fourteen-year-olds when my body was so large. Some things I love to smash.

Love Me for a Reason

I work every day with my friend Pat Jobe, who is perhaps the best at loving people of anyone I've ever met. Pat loves almost everyone he knows. It is inspiring in one way. In another way, it ticks me off. The problem for me is, he loves unconditionally. One morning when he told me he loved me unconditionally, I'm afraid I snapped at him.

"I don't want to be loved unconditionally! I want to be loved for reasons. All my life, growing up, I heard that God loved me unconditionally. I was taught that God loves us in spite of our sinful and unworthy selves, and God loves everyone the same. Maybe that was good news to some people, but I wanted something else from God. I wanted to be loved wildly, passionately, helplessly. I wanted God to delight in me, not to love in spite of my being messy and forgetful and mouthy, but because in my own way, I was fabulous."

"So it's love you for a reason or leave you alone, eh?" Pat said.

"That's it. You heard me. Thank you."

Within the next hour there appeared on my desk an oversized piece of white paper with a long message on it in orange marker. "I love you because . . ." it began, and listed twenty-three wonderful qualities Pat saw in me.

The last sentence was, "I love you because you're fabulous." I cried. I have had that piece of paper up by my desk for nearly two years now. It sustains me when I look at it. I can feel it in a way I never could feel unconditional love.

I know this is probably a deep immaturity on my part. I have been told I'm a brat, and I'm afraid that is true. One thing that might have happened is that my child-mind just accepted certain things so deeply and completely that it has taken me until my mid-forties to look at them and say, "Now wait a minute here!" and start asking questions. I have been well loved and encouraged enough now to ask them out loud, and for that I am profoundly grateful. Now and then, after I ask them out loud, someone comes up to me and says, "I thought I was the only one who wondered that!"

The problem is that people keep encouraging me to say and ask things out loud that shock me inside. Hearing myself say out loud that I don't want to be loved unconditionally, that I want to be loved because of things shocked a deep fearful part of me. "I can't believe you said that out loud!" she hissed. "God is going to be *so mad.*"

But you know what? I ask myself. Who gave me this brain that thinks this way, anyway? If I didn't use the brain and the heart I was created with, then I'm not doing the job I was created for, and creating me would have been a waste of time. So I go on and continue to be this bratty, questioning self, trying to be on this earth to learn to love and be loved, and I say to my shocked inner critic, "Thank you for sharing!" She hasn't figured out a comeback for that one yet. And I say to my beloved Pat, thank you, my friend.

I Feel Lucky

⌣⋮

I tell everybody I'm the luckiest person they'll ever meet.
I'm going to say it 'til it's true. Part of the delicious feeling
I get from claiming to be lucky comes from the knowl-
edge that it would horrify my Presbyterian family.

Talking about luck was frowned upon when I was growing up, and mentioning it could result in a lengthy theological lecture. One afternoon when I was sixteen, I was
walking down the street in Philadelphia with my sister,
and we saw my uncle getting out of his car. This uncle
lived in Pittsburgh, eight hours away, and we didn't know
he was in town. "Wow, isn't it lucky to have run across
you like this," we said. "It's unbelievable! What are you in
town for?"

He drew himself up to his full six feet two, took a deep
breath, and rebuked us, "Luck? Luck? I can't believe I'm
hearing you girls say that. Don't you know there is no
such thing as luck? God is in control of the whole world,
and it is a blessing of Providence that we ran into each
other, not luck."

His father, my grandfather, had been a fundamentalist
radio evangelist, famous in his day for the strength of his
opinions, the power of his preaching, and the rarity of his
self-doubt. It felt almost as though the spirit of his father

had come over him as he heard our heedless use of the word *luck,* and a sermon came pouring out.

Providence, for those of you unfamiliar with the lingo, means that God is in control of everything. Well, not of the bad things . . . well, maybe of the bad things, except that we also believe God is good, so they can't really be bad; they must be useful or disciplinary or, failing that, sent from the forces of evil. But Providence says that even the forces of evil can't send bad things without God allowing them to happen . . . Okay, Providence is a really complicated concept and nobody understands it, but one of the things it meant in my family was that good stuff that happened to you was sent from God and not luck. Luck, after all, comes from the same root as the name Lucifer, so we all know who you're talking about when you talk about luck.

Looking back on it with adult eyes, I think now that my uncle was embarrassed to have been caught in Philadelphia, not having called his brother, our father, to tell him he was coming so they could visit. When we are uncomfortable, or when we feel guilty, we spout off more easily and think less about what we're saying, don't we? My uncle wasn't a lecturing kind of person normally. He was just flat unlucky that we came along in that huge city and ran into him.

Unlucky, now that's harder to explain in terms of Providence. What do you say about someone who can't seem to get a break? He gets sick and while he's at the hospital, his house burns down. A week later he totals his car. What is he if not unlucky? Providentially challenged? I'm trying to imagine somebody writing the blues, twanging those steel strings, trying to work in the line, "I been providentially challenged." It doesn't have the right ring, somehow.

I have always been a person to whom good things happen, and I am deeply grateful for them. Bad things happen to me too, but I don't notice those as much. I don't know if that means I have found a healthy, enlightened way of approaching life or if I'm in deep denial. I don't care which it is. Lucky for me.

Thank You, I'm Going Downhill

꒰

Let me explain something about me and spiritual practice. I stink at it. There is nothing I do serenely day after day, glowing from within, filled with light and peace. The practice of mindfulness, for example, makes me so irritable I have to quit after a minute or two. Washing dishes with my whole focus, breathing into the water, doing a careful job, emptying my mind of all other tasks than this one—Just. Doing. This. One. Thing. Arrrrkkk! My mind and body are happy doing five things at once. I have to find a practice that suits me. Gratitude is one thing that has been working out well so far.

I was on my way down from the mountains on Interstate 26 when, a mile before Saluda, my car's engine turned off. I was going downhill, and for some reason, my spiritual practice of gratitude kicked in.

"Thank you that I'm going downhill," I began, popping the clutch to jump the engine back to life. Nada. When the grade rose again, I coasted to a stop on the shoulder of the road. After trying to start the car two more times, I gave up, got out, and, leaning against the trunk of the car, stood facing traffic.

"Thank you that it's not too hot," I said, making my hand into the internationally recognized telephone symbol, my thumb and pinkie extended, holding it up by my ear.

"Thank you that so many people have car phones now."

"Thank you that I'm not in my pajamas."

I looked down and there was an orange and black butterfly sitting in some grass by the highway. "Thank you for the beauty of that butterfly. Look, there is another one! And another one! They must be migrating. Oh, that one's dead. Uh—thank you that the other ones are alive."

After ten minutes of signaling to passing drivers to call in about me, I started walking to Saluda.

"Thank you that I'm not thirsty," I muttered. "Thank you that I have shoes on I can walk in. Thank you that it's only a mile to Saluda from here. Thank you that I don't have to go to the bathroom. Thank you that it's not raining." After maybe four minutes, I saw a Highway Patrol car coming north, on the other side of the median. I waved to him, and he waved back. "Thank you that the officer saw me. Thank you that he's turning around." He pulled to a smooth stop beside me and motioned for me to get in.

"Thank you that it's so cool in this car, " I continued silently in my head (I'm not nuts). "Thank you that I didn't have to walk to Saluda."

The patrolman told me that the phone lines had lit up with calls about me. "Lotta people have cell phones these days." The nearest towing company was down in Columbus, he told me. It would probably take more than an hour for them to get free and come help me. He was willing to take me to the gas station in Saluda, where there was a pay phone I could use. He radioed the police dispatcher to get a phone number for the towing company. She gave it to him, and I had just enough time to write the number down as we swung into the gas station and jerked to a sudden stop. A huge black truck was barreling right at us; it screeched to a dramatic stop, barely avoiding locking bumpers with the patrol car. It was the tow truck.

"Heard you ask for our number over the radio," the red-headed man said, laughing, sliding out of the cab. "I'd heard the calls about her being broke down, and I was on my way down the road right north of here. Almost beat you. "

I'm the luckiest person I know. Or maybe I have hit upon a spiritual practice with instant results. Either way, I'll take it.

Epilogue

I'm trying not to pout. All things considered, I'm holding up well. A couple of months ago I woke up well before dawn, and I decided to go outside to see the meteor showers. My nine-year-old woke up too, and we went out to the backyard to catch a falling star. We looked to the east, where the woman on NPR said they would be more visible. The sky was dark and clear, the stars were gazing down on us calmly, firmly fixed in their places.

We brushed wet dogwood leaves off the picnic table and sat down. The cold began to seep through our clothes, so we stood up again. Maybe I was wrong about the east. We scanned the sky. All was calm. All was bright. Nothing was falling, swooping, or diving. As dawn began to seep into the sky, we gave up.

I have never seen a falling star, and I don't know what that means. I have the fleeting concern that God likes other people more than she likes me. Looking the wrong way time after time, I have missed them. Distracted by company and conversation, getting up to stir the campfire, scuffing through fragrant pine needles, I'm not looking up when the star streaks across the sky. Are they faster than lightning? Are they tiny as a thread or bold and vivid? Are they clear-edged or are they fuzzy, like comets? Do they look white, or do they make colors as they fall?

In a way, it's a gift not to have seen one because the ones I imagine are perhaps more wonderful than real ones. I can give them a drift as they fall, a streak of pink or gold in their trail; I can add the chiming of bells or a whistling like bottle rockets.

I want to see a shooting star, but I want to see one without having to make a great effort. If I set the alarm clock to wake up in the middle of the night during a meteor shower, got dressed, and drove out into the country, I would feel less like I had been given a gift. Maybe I'm expecting too much magic. Do you know why I expect it, though? Because magic has happened to me over and over.

People say good love takes effort. Getting a good job takes effort, a good spiritual path, good work, good relationships, good conversation, good sex, good music—as a rule, they all take preparation, exertion, imagination, and perseverance in order to shower us with their stars of delight. My jobs, though, have fallen out of the sky, my spiritual path came to me straight out of my genetic memory when I was fifteen years old, and my steps along that path have fed my soul. Good conversations have sparked at unlikely times and places; good friends have backed into my life almost without my realizing they were there until they were already too precious to live without. Good love lit up the sky when I was looking up at exactly the right time and place. There has been effort involved in all of these wonders, but not in proportion to the luck and grace I feel in receiving them.

Deep joy has always been a sudden surprise, a grace note, a kiss from the Universe as I was doing those things I knew to do. Now that I look closely, I see that stars have been shooting above me and all around me. In fact, I have the fleeting concern that God loves me best.

The knowledge that you are reading this book is exploding like showers of light over my head. It makes me grin from ear to ear. I hope these stories have been bits of falling light for you too, and that you were looking up at just the right time.